G O N E

W A L K A B O U T

confessions

of a

new york city

dog walker

M I C H A E L   B R A N D O W

Cover and text design by Matthew Morse

Many names and other identifying characteristics of people
mentioned in this work have been changed to protect their
identities. The communal voice is not intended to presume upon
the memories and experiences of others but to reflect the shared
nature of the event itself, as the author remembers it.

ISBN-13: 978-1-09-327800-2

Also by Michael Brandow

New York's Poop Scoop Law:
Dogs, the Dirt, and Due Process
Purdue University Press, 2008

———

A Matter of Breeding:
A Biting History of Pedigree Dogs
Beacon Press, 2015
Duckworth Overlook, 2016
Hakuyosha Publishing Co., Ltd., 2019

INTRODUCTION

Visitors braving the streets of Manhattan have been known to drift downtown, wandering beyond the warm glow of Times Square's light show that drew them like bugs, then delving westward into dark and difficult territory.

Those daring or foolish enough to venture so far from the familiar brand names flashing across billboards and buildings find themselves caught in a web of old country roads that can be as confusing to them as it is to us seasoned locals. Unlike other neighborhoods on this sometimes orderly island, where parallel streets are neatly numbered and one leads predictably to the next, Greenwich Village tries living up to its eccentric bohemian past with a topography that was spared the totalitarian grid. Navigation is trickier on these narrow, meandering roads that appear unannounced from another era then wind and disappear in all directions. Some are still paved in brick from the days of horses and carriages, sidewalks made of original bluestone slabs predating concrete walkways. Lurking in long shadows of those distant glass towers taking over the horizon are quirky little houses with crooked, peeling porticos, their ancient facades crawling with vines. Drawn by rumors of quaintness, unsuspecting visitors wander into my picturesque corner of a city homogenizing more by the moment. They hit the spot where West Fourth Street, against all logic, crosses West Twelfth, and are faced with a conclusion I do not challenge—they're lost.

Maps have always been pointless in these parts. Hand-held devices and GPS are blunt instruments. Humbled by the charming but treacherous landscape that sucked them in, weary travelers lay all compasses down by the wayside and return to that golden rule: When in doubt, always ask the guy with dogs for directions.

That would be me, the photo op anchored to enough canines and local color to be a buoy for the disoriented drifter. "Here, standing before you," a tour guide might say, "is a live specimen of an urban legend nearing extinction, a real, honest-to-goodness New York City dog walker, the old-school, independent variety, a one-man show who answers to no company boss but might stop to answer your questions." The natural choice for strangers seeking safe haven, I'm visible morning through night in rain, snow, sleet or shine. Driving four to six quadrupeds as skillfully as any coachman of old, I'm a weathered thirty-six-year veteran of this town and look the part. Who better to trust than me with my ruddy leather face that's seen it all, my web of leashes, and knowledge of every inch of this terrain, for help back to your overpriced Midtown hotel, or perhaps some tiny auberge you saw on *Sex and the*

City? I'm a beacon to the wayward who've strayed beyond the beaten path, an international symbol to those stranded in embarrassing spots, an ambulant information booth and unofficial welcome wagon to the world—and a good story for the folks back home—if I can get past that first annoying question the clueless ask in a panorama of accents:

"Excuse me. Where is the Village?"

"You're in it" is my reply to poor souls in need of a walker. They stare in disbelief, wondering if I'm kidding or trying to make fun of them for being out-of-towners.

"What were you expecting?" I resist adding sarcastically because I, too, once stood where they waver. Weaned on the New York of movies and TV, fresh from Times Square and all its fakery, they're expecting the Disney cartoon conception of what a "village" must look like. They're suddenly faced with the real deal and not sure how to react, so I try being educational in as neutral a tone as I can muster.

"How much quaintness do you need?" I stop short of barking. "You wanted some sleepy alpine burg with thatched roofs and cobblestones?" Instead of wearing a T-shirt and jeans, I should be in lederhosen yodeling "Edelweiss."

A recent survey asked people, if forced to make a choice in a matter of life or death, whom they'd save first: a dog or a tourist. Surprisingly or not, forty percent said they'd save the dog even if it meant letting the tourist perish! Rather than send humans home with clichés about those "rude New Yorkers" they brought with their baggage, I tear a page from my crew's prepaid walking time and pause to help these pilgrims in plight. The dogs look excited and alarmed but slowly warm to the approaching aliens. They sense my openness, I think, understanding we're on a diplomatic mission, self-appointed—perhaps imposed—but vital just the same. For my dogs, these brief exchanges are chances for free ear scratches. For the tourists, these impromptu chats are opportunities to learn about real New Yorkers, their real dogs, and the real places we go. For me, putting the misguided back on track is a way to reconnect with the outside world, so important when you've been seated at the center of the universe far too long to keep a healthy perspective. These are the folks you don't usually see in the limelight, the ones left behind when I self-exiled to this crowded but somehow lonely island.

So I share my stories about migrating to New York from another world thirty-six years ago, not through Ellis Island but from the opposite direction, and how the many thousands of dogs in my life have been my guides for these past twenty years of walking. I explain how I learned to survive in a line of work that simply doesn't exist in other cities, not like it does in this intensely pedestrian culture of ours with its special constraints on time and space. I myself would not exist anywhere but New York, where my most unusual journey has given me access to a dimension of humanity, and our companion species, few people ever see. I chronicle the many changes I've seen happen in this town, many of them not for the better, since I debarked in 1982.

Anyone who has the courage and curiosity to visit this place in the first place, then the audacity to stop me in my tracks on the sidewalk and ask a question when I'm busy working, must already have a taste of what it's like to go off the grid, to sail with abandon—to go walkabout.

Meander with me.

CHAPTER ONE

My hand trembled as I inserted the first key. It was as though I'd set off an alarm, that foreboding rumble from behind the door keeping me nervous and alert. I'd only heard tales of the mythical beast inside but had good reason to believe there was a very fat, two-hundred-pound Rottweiler just a couple key-turns away. She didn't sound like she'd be happy to see me. The growling grew louder and the myth, I feared, would soon become a reality.

Sensing a rush of adrenaline, I was about to insert the second key but hesitated, my hand shaking in sync with that vibration set off somewhere deep inside the chest of a testy carnivore. My reputation was on the line, a line I didn't feel like crossing, so I only turned the key halfway. Did I really want to be a hero, especially if my only claim to fame would be trying, perhaps failing, to give a reluctant canine a chance to pee? Thinking about this only weakened my resolve for the mission I'd accepted.

The dog behind the door likely heard a familiar jingle coming up the stairs, an alarm that put her on alert, but my clients are put at ease when I tell them about my key policy. You've heard about people who get presented a key to the city for remarkable deeds? I have my own personal sets for much of downtown Manhattan, and only because so many suspicious New Yorkers have learned, as I'm hoping this giant Rottweiler will, to feel comfortable trusting me. I'd never, not even under torture, give away identities by labeling keys. If I made it that obvious whose were whose, and by chance I left them somewhere, or my apartment was robbed, then the whole neighborhood would be, and I'd be to blame.

Hipsters wear keys attached to their hips as fashion statements. Mine are not ornamental but each of them vital to a dog's welfare, and to my reputation. To the untrained eye, the bunch I carried this particular day, part of the extensive collection I keep in a large wooden box at home, were pretty much indistinguishable one from the next. I've been walking dogs long enough not to need tags or writing of any kind that would betray a sacred trust. Not only do I not divulge the names of my clients, I try not to give away the dogs' names, either, because a clever thief could easily go into my black book and break any secret code I might devise.

Instead, I memorize each point of entry by its shape and color, the distinct pattern of the teeth, or whatever odd items the owners have attached. Sometimes it's Mickey Mouse or a peace sign. Maybe it's a classic "Hang in there!" photo of a wide-eyed kitten encased in a plastic heart-shaped locket. For a couple years after the 9/11 attacks on the World Trade Center, in a brief outburst of patriotism uncommon among cynical New Yorkers, it could have been any one of the thousands of little novelty American flags, in cloisonné enamel on metal, all looking alike and making my job more difficult. Somehow I managed. The two keys I was fumbling for on the morning in question (half-heartedly, because I wasn't entirely sure I even wanted this job) were more obvious than most and easy enough to remember. They had a heavy brass "G" attached.

"G" was for Gracie, the enormous Rottie who, I had good reason to believe, was snarling so menacingly from behind that door. I hoped she wasn't too hard on intruders.

I found myself in this awkward and embarrassing position because this wasn't my typical job. I'd never laid eyes upon dear Gracie or graced her doorstep with my jingling. Gracie and her owners didn't even know me. I was a total stranger and this was a guard dog, so I couldn't blame her for trying to keep me out. Normally, I wouldn't have considered entering a home before first meeting my assignment, no matter what the size or breed, on his or her own turf with the owners looking on. That way, I'm officially accepted and the dog knows it's alright for me to come back when no one else is around.

But this wasn't my typical job. I owed someone a favor. A last-minute call from a sick dog-walking colleague sent me rushing out at that early hour of a summer morning already piping hot, first to pick up the keys from the regular walker, home and bedridden, then to walk the dog that didn't appear to be receiving guests. Even if Gracie had known me, I was told, getting into her space would have been a tricky business. Her owners knew this and always left a survival kit for the regular walker, a big dog biscuit they strapped to the wall with duct tape within easy reach of anyone afraid to enter. An extra-grande Milk-Bone was the peace offering I'd be needing to negotiate safe passage.

When I first got into this line of work, I knew it was a little off-the-wall. Entering apartments when no one's home isn't something most people would feel comfortable doing, whether or not there's a guard dog waiting on the other side of the door. Under normal circumstances, my first arrival in a client's home is for a proper interview, not a test of wills with an animal I've never met. Unlike that tension-packed morning, I already have a foot in the door, and have passed all the right rituals. Not only are the owners there to welcome me and reassure their pets that I'm alright to let in, I come highly recommended by a friend, a dog trainer, a vet or a groomer, or by another dog walker they know from the neighborhood and who swears by me. Word-of-mouth is enough and I've never had to advertise. I'm in the trust business. How much would you pay for that?

In fact the interview, when there is one, is often a mere formality. I probably won't even shave for the occasion because it's not really necessary since I left corporate life and went underground. I used to wear a suit and tie to first encounters, but as a dog walker it's no less important that I dress appropriately and look the part than it was in my cubicle hellhole in the sky. My jeans and T-shirt, though stained with paw prints of all shapes and sizes, and clinging with dog hair from the entire spectrum of black to red to tan to white, are clean by the standards of my trade. My sneakers, though shabby and bottoming out from the constant pounding of pavement—the last pedometer reading was eighteen miles in one day, including the several hundred steps I climbed—are the nicest pair I own.

No one can say I don't look like a pro. Since I dropped out and started my long journey on foot, I've undergone a physical transformation. I have muscles in my legs, arms, shoulders and chest I never thought I'd have. I used to be as skinny as the railing I used to labor up five flights to try and walk Gracie. Unlike so many of my clients who spend endless hours attached to machines at the gym to achieve that rugged, outdoorsy look, I earned mine by keeping large dogs from stepping off the curb into oncoming traffic, and by climbing these stairways to heaven, or hell, depending how it works out for me. It's true, I don't have the standard six-pack abs so highly prized these days. I haven't time or energy left for the gym, and the muscles I have aren't cosmetic. I got them from hard, brutal work, and look strong and healthy because I *am* strong and healthy, more than capable of keeping a big-ass Husky from dragging me down the street, or the stairs.

So far have I drifted from mainstream middle-class Manhattan, so entirely have I been corrupted by the freedom of the street, that sometimes I need to be careful not to go too far. I have enough stubble on my face to describe myself as "scruffy" on dating sites. Museum security guards started following me around when my beard got out of hand, so now I maintain my face with an electric razor at a just-so setting that doesn't say "homeless guy" but gives an unkempt but studied look the French would call *faussement négligé*. It's alright for people to know I'm a little edgy, just not gone off the cliff and dropped out entirely. New clients must be reassured I haven't wandered too far from normal polite society. Otherwise, they wouldn't trust me with their beloved companions, or their keys.

Wearing slightly soiled clothing to an interview is about more than meeting a prospective client's expectations of how a dog walker should look. If I washed my uniform too often, more than the fresh T-shirt I wear daily, I'd be depriving myself of another advantage, and the dogs of a wealth of information. From the moment I try to enter their lives, many dogs develop an almost morbid fascination with my jeans and sneakers. Canine calling cards nearest their reading level, they have imprinted on them, along with the paw prints and dog hair, those invisible marks left in passing, the best recommendations in town.

Each scent paints a picture and every picture tells a story. A few kind words have been left by my dear old friend

Max, the excitable dachshund who jumps on me whenever I arrive to walk him. Another rave review comes from Josie, the Wheaten mix who sits on my lap at the dog run because she's nervous around strange dogs. Bubba the black Lab always rubs against me on the sidewalk, leaving that pungent aroma so typical of his breed, a written confession for anyone wanting to know what other dogs I've been seeing. Elsa the Great Dane licked my shoe after Marge, the Boston terrier, dropped a piece of hot dog treat on my foot and Eunice, her competitive sister, moved in to grab it. I am an open book. The Illustrated Man. Scratch-and-sniff. Every mark is an invitation to come play in my strange and exciting little world. The owners may be leery, but if the dogs give me a paws-up then I've pretty much got that shoe in the door.

In fact I've become a kind of canine cult figure in my neighborhood. Dogs I've never met mob me on elevators. They follow me down the street after catching wind of my tales. Overwhelmed and overstimulated to the point of surrender, they're so utterly taken in that I'm embarrassed to see the hurt expressions on the faces of people whose own best friends, the creatures they've loved and nurtured for years, seem a little too willing to follow me out the door.

Getting a shabby sneaker through a second time isn't always as easy. Some prospective clients ask me to do a trial run—a walk, actually—for which they're more than happy to pay even if they decide to go with someone else. They want to make extra-sure their loved ones are comfortable and safe with me, that I'm in charge but gentle on the leash, and most important: that we're coming back. Some nervous parents join their dogs on that first, introductory outing, just in case I turn out to be a nut. Others have someone else do this on the sly. More than once, a trusty neighbor has been planted on the street below to follow and keep an eye on someone's dog. Exiting the building with leash in hand, I can always spot the snoopers peeping around lampposts, from behind bushes and parked cars, while I pretend not to notice for the length of our promenade. Some walkers are insulted by this. I respect anyone who cares enough about a dog to have me followed, and encourage my clients to be as suspicious as humanly possible. There really are a lot of nuts out there, irresponsible idiots who ought not be entrusted with the center of someone's life, or with their keys.

If the owners are apprehensive about handing over to total strangers the keys to their hearts, some dogs aren't any less shy about subjecting me to their own rites of passage.

They all know the drill. Pavlov couldn't have planned it better. Buzzer goes off. Stimulus sets off a four-legged frenzy with dogs barking, jumping, beside themselves with anticipation. Who, pray tell, is at the door? If a household has more than one ebullient beast, each intensifies the other, building the crescendo of yapping, howling, hopping and scratching to a fever pitch that won't break until someone, anyone, enters that apartment to play this piece out to the end. Canines, like their humans, are creatures of habit and even their most impassioned moments aren't entirely unscripted. Annoyed neighbors already know the plot and are not amused. They've experienced the chaos unleashed when I press the wrong buzzer by mistake, to another apartment with dogs, just not the ones I'm supposed to meet that day. Some pooches won't stop pacing and whining by the door for hours, unwilling as they are to give up hope that someone, anyone, is arriving as promised. They may have to be locked in a back bedroom just to calm down, and to keep the neighbors from banging on the walls.

I gear up for the usual hoopla as the elevator door opens, or I conquer that last flight of stairs in a walk-up building, and begin my final approach down the hall. If I had hair on my back, it surely would be standing now. Crossing a threshold is a moment filled with tension, not so much because I'm nervous about not being liked and losing the job to another walker, but because entering at all is a frustrating exercise in crowd control. Typically, the apartment door flies open to a narrow foyer already packed to the gills with a person trying comically to restrain by the collar at least one dog bouncing off walls and rushing at me as I try to take that slow and gentle first step forward. Sometimes I'm pushed right back into the hall, not because the dogs don't want me, but because they want me too much. These purgatorial moments stuck in entryways are as trying as those New York traffic jams known a "gridlock."

Everyone wants to be somewhere else, no one can advance, and without some heroic gesture of accommodation, no one will anytime soon.

Most dog owners are pathetically inept in these situations and I, being a professional, am the one who must take the reins and re-establish order. Always open to giving a friendly pat on the head or a scratch behind the ears, I extend a hand of friendship, fingers tucked in safely in case a dog has other ideas. I speak in high-pitched baby talk, making little clicks with my tongue and puckering my lips with kissing sounds that melt the hearts of most audiences instantly. I've made sure to memorize each dog's name in advance of an interview, which can come in handy for barking commands like "sit," "off," or "no bite." This all requires diplomacy on my part, and stuck on the other side of that border crossing, I can't resist feeling that I, too, must be on my guard. Any good trainer will tell you, a wagging tail doesn't necessarily mean a dog's happy to see you. A wagging tail is a sign of *excitement*, which can go either way.

First impressions are as important to dogs as they are to humans. It's all about body language, breathing, voice tone, not so much what you say as how you say it. Whatever happens, I mustn't show fear, inappropriate familiarity or forwardness, and my performance must be convincing. "All dogs just love me," says every idiot on the sidewalk. No they don't, not unless they're really stupid. Self-styled "dog lovers" are always waving their arms, rushing up to grab my animals and pet without permission, as any well-trained child knows better than to do. The best intentions in the world won't bury the fact that we're all political animals and must be handled with kid gloves, not to mention treated with respect, unless of course the dog in question is a half-wit golden retriever who will gladly, the owner says proudly, "show a burglar where the silver is."

If the first impression I make in a crowded doorway is a good one, most dogs will settle down in a few seconds. They're calmed by my own natural animal magnetism—or manipulative personality—a quality many people think they have but haven't really cultivated. Admittedly, I'm not always in control, of myself or others. Sometimes I'm having a bad day and feeling insecure or cranky. Dogs sense I'm a little off, less on top of the situation than they are. I might get the job, but my charges may never fully respect me. Far into the future they'll test me, again and again, out of concern, sport, or sheer boredom, each time I come to rescue them from their hours of isolation.

Something as simple as attaching a dog's leash can be a daily challenge, depending on the dog. One difficult border collie named Penny, bored out of her mind and half-crazed in a noisy city where a tightly wound farm dog has no business being, acquired a taste for luring me into the living room, leash in hand, then getting me to coax her from underneath the sofa before she'd consent to taking her midday constitutional. Decidedly dug in, she wasn't budging and I had no choice but to take the bait by kneeling down and fumbling for her collar to drag her out, all the while hoping all five fingers reappeared unsavaged. This game went on for weeks, until one day the bored border collie decided to up the ante. Determined not to make it easy for me, she came rushing out from under the sofa, teeth bared. Leash in hand, I rose sternly to deliver a no-nonsense "No!" and we were on our way. After a few of these daily exercises, she lost interest and decided to push the envelope again. She jumped and nipped while I walked calmly to the kitchen and climbed onto a counter. I called her dad at work to say this wasn't working out.

Now, proud parents don't like being told their precious darlings are poorly behaved, not even when they're downright obnoxious. I tried to explain to this sassy lassie's dad that he needn't be insulted about my update on his pricey, high-strung specimen from a "reputable" breeder, a type bred for generations to live in the country and be tough on sheep, not on dog walkers, to run across rolling green hills, not to pine away the days in a New York apartment and burrow under the sofa, but to no avail. "She's never done that with *me*," the dog's dad testified as I pleaded a simple bite on the leg could be quite serious for me. I'd be out of work without pay, I explained, and who knew for how long.

For all a rich-kid hipster's talk of social justice and universal health care, this type hasn't a clue about how the rest of the world must survive. In prestigious universities, or upscale co-op buildings, they're used to having servants who don't contradict them, just like they had living at home with their indulgent parents. They're constantly apologizing to each other for their "privilege" but think I should be grateful for their money and make no complaints. Perched on the kitchen counter in a lotus position with my cell phone, a spoiled brat's spoiled brat keeping vigil below, I asked my client if he might consider including health and disability benefits with the fifteen dollars he was paying for the half-hour walk. He got the sarcasm and hung up on me, rushing home from his overpaid techie job with flexible hours, "horizontal management," casual Fridays every day of the week, and dogs allowed—every dog but his, because she was a biter. He relieved me of KP duty and patted his snarly little angel on the head, which any trainer will tell you was a reward for bad behavior. He took back his keys, the supreme gesture of haughtiness when you're throwing someone off your property and out of your circle of trust.

I had a feeling that Gracie the supersized Rottie, home alone and standing her ground, would be conducting this interview on her own terms. All my smooth talking, squeaky cartoon noises and cockiness evaporated as I geared up to cross that threshold and tread upon some dangerous ground.

The growling amplified as I inserted the second key into the top lock and turned. Locks, like dogs and their owners, all have their own individual quirks. Years of forcing my way into old, funky New York apartments have given me a knack for jiggling a key just right, rattling the door with the other hand to get the mechanism aligned, then finishing with a smooth, unbroken turn of the wrist that has taken years to perfect. I have so many locks to conquer each day, sometimes several on the same door depending on how paranoid the New Yorker, that I'm bound to get a few that don't cooperate on the first try. They stick stubbornly on hot and humid dog days of August, though Gracie's owners didn't really need locks. I pitied the burglar who tried to break into her home.

Rottweilers became popular back in the seventies when New Yorkers, nerves frayed from an urban crisis, were getting these dogs for both companionship and protection. The city was falling apart. Government was barely able to provide police protection at a time when we had the highest crime rate of anywhere in the world (except for Detroit, where I was born). Something had to be done. Coaxed by home insurance companies that started requiring customers to keep enormous guard dogs if they wanted theft coverage, New Yorkers began taking matters into their own hands. They bought foreboding breeds like German shepherds, Dobermans and Rottweilers, which is where Gracie's ancestors came in. It's no coincidence that Rotties were used in those original *Omen* movies in the seventies. Massive beasts with glowing red eyes protected the spawn of Satan, like Cerberus, the mythical three-headed hound that guarded the gates of Hades. Odd anachronisms like Gracie, descendents of those gladiatorial types no longer practical since crime has dropped to nil, can still be found, in purebred and mixed varieties, in New York apartments like this one where they're still very much on their guard. The new New Yorkers have their flat-faced, mobility-challenged bulldogs and Frenchies, hardly threats to anyone. But people get attached to breeds like they do to brands of soap, and every now and then I come face-to-face with a slice of the past.

Gracie's reputation preceded her. Turning that second lock was like cranking up a subwoofer. The floor vibrated and beams creaked as the dog hopped up and down, her fiendish growl giving way to a roar that penetrated the steel door. I couldn't tell if I was perspiring from the torrid summer heat, or from fear when I heard that fateful click and the door slowly began to open of its own accord. This happens a lot in old and crooked New York apartment buildings where everything's a bit askew and making me feel even less in control of a situation. A blast of icy air hit my sweaty face as I reached my left hand inside, a firm grip on the doorknob with the right to prevent a wider opening, then leaned awkwardly to grope for the survival kit I was promised, that giant Milk-Bone biscuit strapped to the wall with duct tape. I felt it, the only thing dear Gracie would consider in negotiations like this, hanging like a crucifix in the entry. I grabbed it, ripping off the tape along with some paint and plaster. The door started opening by itself again and I was struck by the unmistakable scent of a large, unwashed dog. I could feel the heat of her breath.

Rule number one when you're talking to a proud dog parent: Their dog is the *cutest* one you've ever laid eyes on! Don't get me wrong. I love all dogs, and if I'm self-promoting when I say this, it's only a matter of time until I've grown attached and a lie becomes the truth. Like a politician who starts believing in his own positions, I know that soon every dog in my life will be the cutest one I've ever laid eyes on.

Even the few dogs who give me a hard time at first eventually work their way into my heart. Breeds I never thought I could take seriously as real dogs, much less love, have also won me over. Like the undignified male Yorkie named "Zeus," poofed up with a hair dryer, soaked in perfume, neutered and emasculated, a yappy little thing weighed down with barrettes and ribbons, who could barely jump high enough to pee on the sofa, much less command my respect. This tiny fellow grew on me, and I cried the day we put him down.

Saying I love all dogs is understating my attachments. I adore them. Like many dog walkers, I got into this line of work because I didn't want to deal with my own kind any more than was absolutely necessary, but soon my reasons changed. Oddly enough, I bond with the owners as well. Our shared love for their dogs brings us together. After the interview, and the first few days on the job before unconditional trust sets in, I sometimes won't see the humans for months, even years. What's amazing is how closely we relate on those rare occasions when we run into each other on the street by chance. I'm the guy who tends to the center of their lives each day at the appointed hour while they're away at the office. How much would you pay for peace of mind?

But winning someone over doesn't happen overnight. In the beginning, some clients call me dozens of times each day to make sure everything is working out and their pups are in good hands. The more neurotic ones want me to leave Post-It notes detailing, in lurid, small-print detail, how each promenade unfolded, what adventures we had, what new friends we made. People's private lives are very strange places. The mom of a fluffy white bichon frise leaves me a checklist, specially engraved in fancy script and printed on expensive stationery like a wedding invitation, to record her delicate darling's daily bowel movements and urinary history. How many times did Annabelle go and where? What was the state of the stool: "Hard?/Medium?/Soft? (Please check one.)"

Dog owners can be so interested in that half hour I spend with their best friends that I wonder if they aren't secretly jealous of me for having this quality time with them. My cold, misanthropic heart melts, just a little, at the thought, and I almost feel guilty for doing my job. Every career, no matter how offbeat or rebellious, requires compromise. Any routine can change you in subtle ways. I do what makes the owners happy and keeps them loving their dogs, no matter how pointless or absurd their emphatic instructions, so long as the dogs aren't being harmed.

"Bonzo likes to be told to go to the window and search for flies before he goes out for walkies," says the owner of a tightly wound fox terrier while explaining my daily duties. Sure enough, Bonzo won't go out before being commissioned to hunt down insects on the windowpane, though whether he was taught this behavior or decided for himself remains a mystery.

"Petey knows the difference between *cookie* and *grape*," claims the owner of a pug who seems to require, not only a reward after every poop and pee, but a preview of what form the prize will take.

I did things far more ridiculous and demeaning when I had a corporate job.

"Sophie just loves her little snookies," says a woman who returns to childhood each time she hugs her cocker spaniel mix—and so do I.

Gracie, a dog of a different color, had her own idiosyncrasies, as I was about to learn and hopefully live to tell about. Her hair-raising howl stopped when the door, slowly opening as though driven by some spirit, approached the point of no return but stopped halfway, wedged into the doorframe of that very crooked old New York apartment building.

A half-confident push revealed that enormous anachronism from another era, the biggest, fattest Rottweiler I'd seen in all my years of dog walking. Gracie was parked about two yards in front of me like a tank on Tiananmen Square, looking straight at me and nearly silent after all those loudspeaker warnings leading to this standoff. Her eyes weren't glowing red, not like in the horror films, but they had a certain intensity. Her growl was puttering, like those lawnmowers I remember from my previous life in the suburbs, the ones that ran a few seconds after you cut the gas. Gracie hadn't yet decided if she should sink her teeth into my leg and disable me for life, or simply enjoy her Milk-Bone and go outside for a pee like a good girl. Such are the choices life presents us.

Rather than approach and accept the dog biscuit I offered with a trembling hand, Gracie stepped backward into the apartment, the dry hardwood floor, finish worn bare from years of passing paws, moaning under her weight. I followed her into one of those bizarre New York kitchens you don't see much anymore, this barrel of a beast practically filling the tiny space which doubled, actually tripled as a kitchen, dining room and bath with a tub in the center. A sheet of plywood balanced on top of the tub, covered with a tablecloth and flanked by two unmatched chairs. The floors were severely slanted, as were the shelves and counters. There didn't seem to be a single right angle in this place where doors opened by themselves then stopped halfway. A disorienting stage set for some German

Expressionist film, lines going off at all angles, also typical of this vintage New York kitchen was the fact that nothing was hidden. Unlike the new refurbished spaces, upscaled with shiny, flush surfaces and nothing utilitarian in sight, a dishrag and flyswatter hung unapologetically from crude rusty nails on a wall cracked and distressed with no designer's help. Sloping, doorless shelves made of unpainted wood displayed a box of oatmeal, a bag of flour, jars of jam, cookies, potato chips, tins of tea, pots, pans, dishes, cups, glasses and silverware, all in plain view and covered with the dust of the ages, about to come sliding down in an avalanche of kitchen gadgets. The tawdry scene showed how many people still live in this town. We kick and claw at each other to call these places our own, and are grateful to get them at any price. The informality and lack of pretense of interiors is a reminder that a New York apartment is not so much a home as a refuge from our very communal lives in shared public spaces. The dumps we occupy are caves stuffed with whatever we can fit, dens we burrow into at the end of the day to lick our wounds.

Surveying the hovel that Gracie called home, a cave not very different from mine, I grabbed the brown leather leash off the counter and got on my knees—my instructions were to avoid hovering which she found threatening—and started speaking in baby talk, a trick that gets a response from most dogs. "Come here, girl," I pleaded in that soft, high pitch known to soothe the savage beast. Gracie just stood there as I groveled like an idiot. She wasn't in the least bit interested in the biscuit I clutched like a weapon. Losing faith in those opposable thumbs for which my species is famous—perhaps an overestimated trait—I slowly opened my grip on the treat, letting it balance on a sweaty palm for her to take if she pleased.

I was told by Gracie's regular walker to avoid too much direct eye contact, something else a dog of her temperament finds offensive. Focusing on the run-down hardwood floor, I grasped the leash in one hand and served the peace offering with the other, fingers tucked away, just in case. This dog was a pro. She'd played this game many times before and knew exactly what I was up to. Her nostrils flared. She wanted to show how little she cared about me and my pathetic Milk-Bone, but started drooling beyond her control. Determined not to be a cheap date, she resisted taking the path of least resistance and turned around, disappearing down the hall.

Great. Was I ever going to get this dog, and all the others waiting in their respective crooked spaces, out for walkies? I entered the bedroom and slid a hand along a wall for a light switch that wasn't there. This was one of those dark, dreary, rear-facing New York apartments where you can't tell if it's day or night without looking at a clock, or know the weather outside without checking The Weather Channel. My eyes took a few seconds to adjust to the unlit room and I drifted toward the sound of Gracie's heavy breathing. She was in the closet.

I was only getting paid fifteen dollars for a half-hour walk and already I'd spent ten minutes trying to get near this dog. Lesser walkers would have turned back at this point. Most would never have made it through the front door. I didn't want to be a hero, but owed someone a favor and needed to get this dog out, even if she didn't want to go. Some of the sleazy walkers might have lied and said they walked her but didn't. There was no doorman in this building to report back to the owners. This is done all the time, and more out of laziness than fear. Another trick is to lie about how long you kept the dog out, doing fifteen minutes and getting paid for thirty. The dogs aren't going to tell, though in recent years some owners have installed webcams on the sly.

Giving up so soon was not my style, and in all honesty, I was still enjoying the perverse pleasure of that adrenaline rush. Gracie's regular walker assured me she'd never actually hurt anyone, just given them food for thought for years to come.

I leaned precipitously into Gracie's clothing-closet retreat. Her eyes glowed, almost like in the horror movies, through something made of sheer fabric, and the scent of mothballs made me queasy. Extracting a dog from such a tight spot is a tricky business, but I had my own method tried already on smaller dogs. The technique worked well with a miniature apricot poodle named Buster who tries to bite anyone, including his owners, presumptuous enough to want to put a leash on him. It's the hands that set him off, and it's not his fault. He was rescued from death row at a pound Upstate, and his fear of being handled likely comes from abuse at a previous owner's hands. When I first reached to attach the silver lamé leash to this rehomed pup's matching designer collar, he snapped and I pulled back to rethink my plan. Funny thing is, Buster the reluctant apricot poodle actually likes being leashed, once he is. Attached and subdued, he turns from snarling and menacing Hyde into sweet and cuddly Jekyll.

How would I convince Gracie to grow attached to me? Just like I did with Buster, I took her leash and made a kind of lasso through the looped handle at one end before even thinking of reaching into that closet hideaway. Gracie's glowing eyes as my guides, I dangled my impromptu snare like a fisherman lowers his net. Leaning into the closet headfirst, bracing myself on the doorframe, I reached close enough to encircle her massive neck, barely visible in silhouette through a chiffon skirt. Gracie's growling resumed, frustrated as she was at being cornered, aware this game of hers was coming to an end. I gave the lasso-leash a light swing away from her, then let it come down around her neck. A gentle pull, and the tension I felt meant I had her!

This was the same tension a dog feels when we're walking. In a way, we're both attached to the same leash, and like most everything else in life, this is a negotiation. Dogs seem to enjoy knowing I'm there at the other end and in control of the situation, however much I struggle to keep them from getting into any mischief they seek. They pull, if not trained, to get close to other dogs, lampposts, or dropped chicken-wing bones ahead, but the tautness reminds them I'm not far behind. The same for harnesses, or snugly-fitting sweaters and coats: some dogs are much calmer in them. Restraint seems to ground them, and certain types, like Huskies, thrive on that resistance, leaning into it as though pulling a sled. For dogs with this drive, it's a pleasure to pull, but you need something to pull, even if that something is me.

The moment Gracie felt me at the other end of the leash, she became a new dog. She stopped her naughty growling and her whole body was relaxed and enthused. I pulled my rodeo lasso to keep her in check, reaching around with the other hand and attaching the leash to her collar. The loop slipped off her neck and we were ready to go!

The dog who, minutes ago, had looked like she wanted to take a chunk out of me was suddenly the puppy her owners still remembered. She jumped up and down—as high as this fat girl could, pictures on the bedside table rattling—darted from the closet, and dragged me into the kitchen where she loaded up on water from her ocean of an aluminum dish. Slobbering across the floor as she went, she snatched the biscuit I'd dropped, then walked nicely by my side down the stairs.

Like me, Gracie understood that taking a fiercely independent stance in life is tempting, and an admirable thing to do, but if you can't strike some arrangement that works both ways, you won't get far.

CHAPTER TWO

The tourists may be drawn to my handsome hounds and remember me as that nice New York dog walker who stopped
and gave them directions to the most charming little café. Still
I seriously doubt that any of them would want their own children to follow my career path.

What made someone like me, educated, connected, a
person with other opportunities in life, settle for being a dog
walker? The lowest of the low, status-speaking, one step up
the curb from street cleaner in the eyes of many, a handler of
excrement—I'm sure that's the question they're holding back,
or might look back and wish they'd asked once safely returned
to their lives.

Not to brag, but this poor little rich kid who went off
the grid comes from a very posh place. An elite suburb of
Detroit, our kingdom counted its average per capita income
among the highest, right up there with Manhattan's Upper
East Side, Greenwich, and the hills of Beverly. My two sisters
and I were the *jeunesse dorée*, or gilded youth, as the French say.
We had prep schools, riding clubs, piano lessons, cars, motor-
cycles, stereos, ski trips, a television in every room—the finest

"purebred" dogs money could buy—all the perks a snob needs to feel a breed apart from the rest of humanity, and to feel safe from the world. Having relations who still occupied "the other side of the tracks" didn't keep us from believing it was all some sort of birthright that no one could take away, even though we ourselves were social climbers who'd only just moved in with the folks on the hill.

My adoptive father, a kind and generous self-made man who came from terrible poverty but worked his way "up" in the postwar years when the world was America's oyster, once confessed to me what pushed him to succeed. Raised in a tar paper shack with newspapers on the walls to keep warm, he said, he wanted more than anything to have a fine house with a big, manicured front lawn greener than cash to call his own. The ever-expanding list of essentials to luxury, prestige, and "keeping up with the Joneses" inevitably followed, but that front lawn, simple and honest, was what started my father's uphill climb.

Our house was extravagant but by no means a mansion, except maybe in a *poor* person's eyes. This was before the endless rows of "McMansions," so common these days they don't even stand out, though we had all the signs of lavish expenditure. Actually, that front lawn wasn't so basic, but grandiose and wasteful, as was our opulent arch of a circular drive like the one on the *Beverly Hillbillies* show. Bloomfield hillbillies? Alongside us were similar properties, one after the next, elegant, rambling homes with facades in very different styles but inhabitants like us with appearances to uphold and cash to burn. A local ordinance in our hoity-toity township, the one that gave secluded lakes, private clubs and bespoke haberdasheries names like "Kingsley," "Fox and Hounds," and "Country Squire," forbade lowly McDonald's and Burger King from marring the English country landscape. Fences, too, were strictly frowned upon, separating as they would our great lawn from the next and bringing to mind those pathetic boxed-in yards of the working class. Having no visible divisions created an unbroken expanse of rolling green, and the illusion of a single vast country estate of some landed gentry, when in reality we were but one of many front-lawn sharecroppers.

We had it all, but I don't come from the sort of family that leaves things behind. Dad was never trying to found a dynasty, just give us what he'd never had, including a good start. He spent his money like many first-generation rich people, and he counted on me to do the same, to want that big front lawn with the same passion. As far as an entitled brat could see, I already had the lawn which wasn't so special, certainly not worth sweating my life away watering, fertilizing and cutting, then paying sky-high taxes on the soil underneath.

About a year after I left to pursue, on borrowed time, a gentleman's education at a fine university in a subject of little practical value apart from social, my perspective on cushy green carpets began to change. Two former classmates from my prep school, still boys with futures that needn't have been so bleak, gave up all hope of staying with the folks on the hill. One boy from my graduating class hanged himself in the basement for his mother to find. The other was a year behind me. I gave him rides to school every morning. "I'm used to a certain standard of living," he always said while handing over a few bucks as his share of the gasoline money, perhaps worried he might not have the grades, or guts, to amass capital, or credit, as our clever fathers had done.

They found him in a field where I used to ride my motorcycle. The family's Lincoln Town Car was parked there, engine idling, a garden hose connecting the exhaust pipe to the deluxe leather interior.

Immigrating to faraway New York City, a place most Americans couldn't even find on a map and where not many people have yards, was a logical move for a young gay man with aspirations outside the norm. This was a viable alternative to suicide, in one form or another, which might have been my fate had I stayed in that posh Michigan suburb. Sure, I could have been a rich hairdresser to all the idle housewives in town, maybe even kept the manicured front lawn. I could have been a fabulous interior decorator, or official architect to our provincial aristocracy. Somehow I knew there was a world of other opportunities in New York, different ways to live I'd never thought of, a new perspective for myself. I'm still not rich like my parents wanted, but escaping that preppy upper-middle-class heaven—hell to me—was a matter of survival.

This pilgrim's progress wasn't always a straight line, and many times I had to stop, check my bearings, and reset my course. Seems like ancient history now, that long lunch break I took, my one-way walk from a miserable corporate job in a shiny glass tower high above Midtown Manhattan. Lowering myself to office work was a way to fund my writing, even to write on company time when things were slow, but each year the trade-off was making less sense.

For fellow inmates who really wanted to be trapped in that dreadful place, because they lacked other talents or aspirations—or had learned to leave those, along with their diplomas in real subjects, in the past and on the counter—staying perched up there in the sky was a point of pride, a new source of identity, a chance to use the royal "we" and pretend they still had higher purposes.

The typical strategy for most corporate executives to keep their self-respect is to have families, and then to suddenly claim they're doing it all for them. Suspiciously convenient, I think, and just the way to give their employers the ultimate choke collar on them, this is the perfect strategy for absolving themselves of all responsibility—for whatever awful things their companies are involved in, and all the indignities they suffer—because anything they do from this point forward is "for the kids."

All but the wisest of poor souls I left hanging themselves in those lofty cubicles saw my exit as the eccentric act of an unbalanced loner, selfish and decidedly a step down in life. An affront to everything they represented, leaving a good job to be a dog walker was not something a "quality" person from a "good" family would do. It made me look kind of crazy. For years, my parents were embarrassed and ashamed beyond belief, and they tried to keep the news of my leap from respectability hidden from friends and relations back in our uppity Michigan town. "Michael's doing fine in New York City," they kept reporting. "He just loves his job." How could I trash a fine education—never really needed, let's be honest, for that mindless corporate routine I dared to turn up my nose at—to toil my life away as a manual laborer? What about everything my father had worked for?

To those with sights set higher—or lower?—my actions made absolutely no sense. No matter to the status-conscious that I'd doubled my income by leaving the bank, because that was not the point of having a decent job, try as I did to explain to my parents who just didn't see it my way. No more than my bosses deserved to "earn" those lavish bonuses, however poorly their company performed and whatever damage their shenanigans did to the economy, because this was more about prestige than money. It wouldn't have mattered if I were a millionaire dog walker—or would one day became a famous dog-walking author—because my career move was a personal insult to all implicated and not easily forgiven.

This wasn't just any corporate job I'd thrown away without consulting anyone for advice. I was glorified secretary to the board of the largest bank in the world, and advancement was offered. For reasons most people could not comprehend, I chose picking up poop on the lowly sidewalk over breathing a rarified atmosphere atop Mount Olympus with the fabled Masters of the Universe.

My only regret is having squandered so much time in society's good graces before scrounging up the courage to start actually doing something with my life. After sixteen years of dry rot in the inner sanctum, supporting some of the world's most senior corporate leaders, the last few years spent reflecting on the question and hesitating before taking my leap, I still didn't know what, exactly, anyone actually *did* up there in those clouds above Midtown Manhattan. I used to say under my breath that my bosses were "paper pushers," a term that needs updating in a nearly-paperless environment. The parasites use new devices now, but still collect sky-high compensation that would make most noses bleed. Spreaders of rumors and setters of benchmarks, they move mountains of capital in a few short keystrokes. Obscenely overpaid courtiers, they glide on wheeled ergonomic *chaises*, like Louis XIV floated about Versailles on the backs of servants, through indoor gardens, expensive artwork, and high security. Dignitaries travel from all points of the globe to pay their respects, to jump on the latest buyout bandwagon, debt restructuring, or whatever fashionable financial "tool" they've just invented to keep everyone guessing. Impersonating workers who actually *do* something for a living, necks secured with horsey Hermès ties for the men, and scarves for the women, in rope-and-stirrup motifs, the great financiers offer strategic advice and launch campaigns, not from the perspective of a common foot soldier or a groom, but with the noble stance of an equestrian class.

Leaving all that to drive my coach-and-four-or-more down the sidewalk would be the smartest move I'd ever make. When the real estate bubble crashed in 2008, largely the fault of the very people I worked for, and so many expendable bureaucrats were laid off, I saw just how much all that "job security" was really worth. The house-of-cards came crashing down, and former co-workers started calling *me* for work.

In the meantime, having jumped the gun on downward mobility, confined to the pavement like a fallen angel, I had some adjusting to do. I stopped shaving and learned to spit on the sidewalk with as much gusto and precision as the grittiest of manual laborers. My body grew heavier but lean and strong. My suits went to charities because they no longer fit—I had no place to wear them, anyway—and Levis, T-shirts and comfortable shoes became my new uniform. Calluses formed on my hands and feet. My face tanned and roughened like the Marlboro Man's. My eyes sharpened like an eagle's. Free from the petty politics, mindless distractions, and numbing routines of corporate life, I grew keenly aware, from great distances, of dangers to my dogs. Without looking, I sensed the ebb and flow of traffic, human and machine, the mass of cars, buses, and trucks, remembering to look both ways for bikes whooshing by less easily noticed. Once I learned the ropes and my body accepted this brutal line of work, when not focused on the pavement, I walked with my head held high for the first time in years.

My timing was a bit off. I decided to "drop out" about forty years after that was a fashionable thing for privileged people with other opportunities to do. The times they had a-changed since the sixties, and downward mobility was no longer a socially-acceptable form of self-expression. Here I was, a true eccentric, not making some political statement, crying for attention, or passing through a phase, but going off the grid to keep my sanity, maybe even my desire to stay on the planet. Though I'd never redo it any other way, society didn't make my new career path any easier than the hard concrete was merciful on my knees. After a few months of free-flying below radar, I stopped bothering with social gatherings because they were pointless. Despite the appearances of merry reveling and cutting loose, parties are seldom just for fun in this town, and I doubt they ever were, not even in the free-spirited sixties. Pleasure is always mixed with business when everyone's constantly self-promoting.

"What do you *do*?" is the first question wild-and-crazy partiers ask to size you up and see what your friendship might *do* for them. I was never comfortable with the "do" question, and now, as far as anyone was concerned, "doo" was what I picked up for a living. Conversations stopped in a New York minute. Invitations got lost in the mail. Casual acquaintances dropped like flies. My oldest and closest friends never left or laughed at me, it's true, but they couldn't help smiling that night after dinner, at a shabby-chic locale called Café Loup, when I reached into a back pocket for my wallet—and unfurled a roll of poop bags instead.

Make no mistake. Anything worthwhile or off the beaten path comes with a price, especially free-flying which is hardly for free. Sometimes on those torrid, deadly dog days of August, dragging myself and crew across scorching-hot pavement that radiates misery, I find myself gazing up nostalgically at those air-conditioned glass towers far away on the horizon. The sick longing passes soon enough when I recall how stifling those offices were inside. I've dared to venture where others don't dream to go, and learned there's more to life than physical comfort. In fact my sidewalk vantage has given me insights into the nuts and bolts of how this town actually works, knowledge you don't get chained to a desk in the sky like Prometheus ordering in lunch.

Let's not forget: The city that never sleeps is also the city of shows. Let's also remember: Staying late at the office to do more of nothing doesn't mean you're getting more done. Having lived on high, I can tell from the sidewalk when they're gearing up for another synchronized aerial performance. Returning my final group of dogs at the day's end before retiring to spend some time writing, I know when the owners are planning to walk that extra mile, and to let me do the walking. The writing will have to wait. Calls start arriving around six p.m. from clients who've accepted the fate of being stuck at the office until god-knows-when and I'm called into service for a second, unscheduled outing. Could I also feed Boomer and Bailey, and change the water in their bowls? Never a problem for my furry friends.

I see it coming even before the frantic texts start arriving. Legions on bicycles, with deliveries summoned from aloft, fly by me on the street. Hermeses for hire—messengers, not neckties—they're also working late. They pass with sandwich trays to be signed for on corporate accounts, and documents to be signed. Where, exactly, this city-wide frenzy is first set in motion is hard to pinpoint. Somewhere above Midtown or Wall Street, an IPO is being planned or a new line is launching. "Steve Martin wants to write," a Jack Russell terrier's mom calls to say. "Can you take Mookie for a second walk?" Suddenly the whole town is busy brainstorming and had better cancel any dinner plans. Stacking every floor of those high-rises with some higher purpose, management is under pressure to increase "productivity"—a substance the experts still can't quite agree on how to define or measure—and the moving-and-shaking becomes contagious.

Waves of mass hysteria spread across companies and entire industry sectors, and by the time Boomer or Bailey needs to pee again, the whole world is stuck late at the office. The sun sets while I return unexpectedly to dogs dropped off a few hours before, but on those unplanned evenings the tall glass towers stay ablaze from within, advertising to the world, and to each other: "*We* are working late tonight. *We* are competitive. *We* are professionals and can sit it out longer than you can." To be fair and honest, all this posturing is good business for me, and for my fellow manual laborers, all of us parasites to the parasites. It's how this town keeps going and how we all get paid.

Dog walking is the first paying job I've ever taken seriously. The lives of this turnkey's dogs don't stop when schedules change. Lonely, loving pups must be walked, fed, watered, hugged and talked to when no one's home. Tonight I get paid to be the good guy, the stand-in behind the door when they're expecting their moms and dads. Their disappointment passes soon enough with an unplanned adventure, another romp with their friends from the day.

CHAPTER THREE

For months leading up to my great escape from a corporate cubicle high above Midtown Manhattan, I'd been using my lunch hours to build a following of dogs to lead down the sidewalk. As my pack and pride grew, so did my lunch hours, becoming hours and hours, inspiring gossip in my absence and raising eyebrows when I finally returned, sometimes the next morning. Begging for a severance package, as many co-workers were getting in those troubled times, I learned the bank was not about to play that game and my break would have to be clean.

Well, as clean as the break could be after I'd returned each day with my face tanned, hair windswept, lungs full of fresh air, suit and tie covered with dog hair and paw prints, wearing an impudent smile for those who'd ordered in their lunches to keep up appearances and who glared at me disapprovingly. Finally came the day when doctor appointment excuses were exhausted, and blaming subway delays only delayed the inevitable. Now was the time to sink or swim, to jump or fall—whatever image works—to make a decision that would alter the course of my life, or send me back, tail between my legs, to those co-workers with their smug sense of propriety, their false sense of security, their tolerance of meaningless tasks, and the pain of what-might-have-been forever a thorn in my side.

Defining moments are just what they're called. Do not take these lightly. At precisely noon on that historic day, I left everything on my desk but a picture of my own sweet dog Samantha. I took my first confident step on the road to freedom, never to look back again. It really was that easy, at least for a time. For months, the arrogance of that moment was fuel to propel me. I wore an even bigger smile plastered across my face, so broad it must have seemed obnoxious to passersby on the sidewalk. Fear of change, of financial insecurity—of what others might think—hold back most people from getting out of their ruts and doing something else with their lives, and from ever feeling so bold and wonderful as I did. Shedding those fears was only part of what was ahead, I knew, but jumping each hurdle added inspiration and made me bolder.

My first test came soon enough. One afternoon, a week after I'd taken charge of my life, I was crossing town along East Thirteenth Street holding leashes to three of my original clients. Dear friends, Max the dachshund and the two crazy Boston terriers named Marge and Eunice, followed trustingly as I glanced up at the bright blue sky of a perfect spring day and took a breath so exhilarating it still gives me goose bumps, twenty years later, to recall. Something as simple as leading my friends westward from the East Village made me feel more alive and alert than I'd felt in years. So much about the sidewalk, now my place of employment, seemed different from this fresh perspective. The Village was quieter during the day when nine-to-fivers were at work. Every detail was exposed in crystal-clear air and bristling with newness, like cracks in the pavement and leaves on trees, tulips popping from holes in the concrete, graffiti on trash cans, crooked street signs and weather-worn frames of shop windows. New York street scenes stood out in sharp relief like those hyperrealist airbrush paintings I'd seen in Soho galleries, works that had somehow seemed more real than the real deal.

Not today they wouldn't. I rose from collecting a small deposit from Max, the good boy who'd just done his business not in the house, and noticed something all-too-real was approaching from behind us. A large engine was drawing close, and my dogs were trembling, as I'd seen them do when storms were near.

I cocked my head, keeping a firm grip on my three dogs' leashes, to see a van, spray-painted black, the creepy kind without windows in back, charging up over the curb, about to plow right into us. Dropping the parcel I'd just collected and risking a fine, I pulled my wards quickly toward a building and behind some trash cans, our only option in a pinch. The van didn't slow down, but leaped and landed on the sidewalk, skidding toward us and crashing sideways against the trash cans, trapping me and my dogs against an iron fence.

The four of us were startled but unharmed and safe, for the moment, though we couldn't move. At my head level, through the open window on the driver's side, barely two feet away and face-to-face with me, was the confused and terrified driver of the van. I wanted to scream at him for his stupidity, a Chinese guy probably making deliveries and clearly not knowing how to drive. He kept pressing his foot on the gas pedal, maybe thinking it was the brake, or the clutch. "Take your foot off the fucking gas!" I shouted. He didn't understand. The engine roared, and through the haze of exhaust clouding my crystalline spring day, the driver's eyes were wild and desperate, his teeth clenched and face contorted in pain and helplessness. His eyes locked with mine, and though he couldn't speak English, I knew he didn't mean for this to happen, but he didn't know how to make this stop. A few seconds felt longer. The stranger turned the steering wheel, burned some rubber, and sped off, to where I have no idea.

So much for my new free-spirited lifestyle. What an initiation this was, and what a welcome wagon: Death Van. Years later, I still stop to look at cloud formations, to listen to leaves blow in the wind, savoring my freedom when out with dear friends whose lives are in my hands. Like I said, this is the first paying job I've ever taken seriously, and to keep my dogs safe is a professional oath. I'd throw myself in front of a semi if need be. I must confess, my noble-sounding motives aren't all altruistic, but partly inspired by an instinct of self-preservation. If anything ever happened to one of my dogs, and I broke the heart of a mom or dad, the weight of my actions would be too much and I could never live with myself again.

Sometimes the stress gets to me. Over the last twenty years, I've grown a thick layer of rough, wind-burned, sun-damaged skin, a road map where all routes lead to precancerous growths, but not tough enough to shield me from bad thoughts. In fact since I got into this line of work, I've tossed and turned over a recurring nightmare. It's always the same story, though no less upsetting each time.

In the dream, I'm at the local dog run in Washington Square Park, leashing a gang of four or more. These aren't particular dogs I can identify, but together they cover the whole spectrum of shapes, sizes and coat colors. Their paid romp is coming to an end and each dog looks contented, more relaxed than when arriving an hour before. They've had their run around the trees, greeted old friends and made new ones, sniffed their fill of butts. On the pebbled ground tennis balls are dropped for the next shift to add their slobber and mark as their own. Any sticks not yet eaten are reluctantly released. Wound up but resigned to the fact that we're leaving, my wards cast wistful glances upward at squirrels whose perverse pleasure is to taunt them from low-lying branches. "Wait until next time," all eyes seem to say.

We pass through twin steel gates and my friends' off-leash freedom is officially over, until I drop them, one by one, at their respective homes, detach their collars and say good-bye. I've left the last of my crew, but closing the apartment door realize, oddly enough, I'm still in possession of a leash with no dog attached. How could this be? There's no collar at the other end, so it's unlikely this dog, whichever dog this is, slipped away on the sidewalk without my noticing. Maybe I deposited one dog and, not thinking, walked away with his leash in hand.

Or maybe this leash belongs to a dog I brought to the run—*then forgot to bring home with the others!*

How in hell will I explain this to the owners? *I left their dog in the park?* Panic wastes no time setting in and I'm running back frantically down Fifth Avenue toward Washington Square, leash dangling behind me, desperately hoping to find this dog, whichever dog this is, safely inside the chain-link fence, seated nervously beyond the twin gates, tail wagging as I approach, overjoyed I've come back after all.

But the dream ends badly. I arrive to find the dog run empty, a sea of bone-white pebbles as lifeless as a Japanese rock garden. The dog, whichever dog this was, is gone forever. I'm ruined as a person anyone would trust. My conscience will never be clear. A creature in my care has met some terrible fate and it's all my fault. I wake up in a sweat.

Not to worry: I've never lost a dog in real life, though I've had some close calls. I used to sit for two very sweet Jack Russell terriers belonging to a famous chef named S with a restaurant in the neighborhood. Actually, I was hired by the chef's kept girlfriend who drank too much and seldom seemed to have enough money to pay me when the time came. Often she'd go through her allowance and have me return the dogs to the restaurant instead of their home. They licked their chops as she loaded me with shopping bags full of everything for the menu that day—raw lamb shanks marinated in rosemary and garlic, entire sage-infused pork roasts, white fava bean salad, the most amazing poached artichokes I'd ever tasted, anything she could poach from the restaurant kitchen while her boyfriend the chef was out—bartering with me while the staff looked on helplessly and she raided the icebox to settle her account.

At first I watched only the first Jack, or rather "Rocco," while the kept girlfriend was travelling and the chef was too busy to keep him. Then came the call asking if I could board two dogs, adding a new puppy whose name I can't recall. I couldn't remember it back then, either. Both Jacks were with me a full day, and still I was embarrassed to ask. So I called the trainer who'd referred me for the job and pleaded: "What is this puppy's name?"

"It's probably 'No!' by now," the trainer answered, laughing and letting me go on guessing.

I doubt even the puppy knew his own name yet, though it might have come in handy on our first walk together. Not long after the kept girlfriend had handed off her dogs, Rocco, No!, and three others were with me on a busy cross street and I felt a tug on a leash. No!'s had snapped and the puppy darted down the sidewalk toward a dangerous intersection and the jaws of oncoming traffic.

I've learned a lot about myself by looking after thousands of dogs, each as precious as the next and needing guidance in the city where leashes are lifelines. In times of crisis, when lives are in the balance and every second counts, a heavy calm comes over me, a sort of survival mechanism. I become extremely focused, methodical and calculating, not out of control with emotion but as cold as ice. Instinct told me that running after that puppy would only drive him further toward a fate I did not want to imagine. So I stayed put. I crouched on the pavement, nonchalantly as though nothing was wrong, then began whistling softly and making squeaky noises to the other dogs who wagged their tails and huddled around me playfully. No! stopped in his tracks about twenty yards ahead, his ears pricked high, almost comically seen from behind, then turned and came running back with the kind of unbound enthusiasm puppies have. He'd sensed something fun was going on with the other dogs and didn't want to miss out. I grabbed No! and had him share a leash with his brother Rocco. Examining his own leash, I noticed it was chewed in several places, no doubt why it had snapped. Had this poor pup been walking with his mom who'd let him chew it, he could have been a goner. Now I always check a dog's gear before any handoff, never trusting a nonprofessional not to give me faulty equipment.

I used to take care of another dog, a tightly wound type demanding special care, a miniature pinscher named "Fly." I actually fostered the fashionable time bomb of a tyke in my Village apartment for a year. Fly had been an impulse purchase by J—one of the "Fly Girls" on the show *In Living Color*—a dog cast off and taken by her hairdresser who hired me to walk him but who also decided not to keep him because he was just too hard to handle. The orphan needed another temporary home and I agreed, not knowing how difficult he would be. Fly's was a familiar story. Did he come from one of society's "reputable" breeders who produce very troubled animals, or was he from a puppy mill? It really wouldn't have made a difference. Most likely, his mother was also his sister, and apart from being badly inbred and not quite right in the head, he had spent his formative months in a small cage, and probably more time in the window of one of the chic local pet shops patronized by celebrities because the owners tell the press "We don't sell dogs from puppy mills."

Coming from this sort of social background, Fly was used to peeing and pooing where he slept, a dirty habit normal dogs naturally abhor and quickly learn to avoid. He was constantly wetting and soiling himself when confined to his crate, and didn't seem to mind. The only alternative was to give him free rein in my apartment when I wasn't there. Left to roam, he got right to work antiquing my furniture, rewiring my appliances, going through my books voraciously. Each day I returned to assess the damage and found my other boarders, and my own dog Samantha, huddled on the sofa sheepishly as if to say: "It wasn't us!"

I've never lost a dog in the city, though I've come close, and I've never lost one in the country where I've also come close, just not in a way anyone would imagine.

One weekend I drove Fly with five other four-legged friends to a mountain retreat I discovered Upstate and craved as much as my dogs did. I hoped this would help Fly relax and be better balanced. The natural setting was beautiful and restorative, and a long hike was just what Doctor Michael ordered, but the seedy old motel where we bedded, nestled in a depressed welfare town in the Borscht Belt, had known better days. Rooms had the rare attraction of allowing dogs. Requiring dogs would be more accurate, and every unit reeked of disinfectant. Walking past any door was like setting off a security alarm inside. Late one evening, I purposely traversed the entire length of the motel's disintegrating front porch, past every crooked room number, to hear what would happen. One after the next, dogs joined the swelling chorus that erupted, and lights clicked on inside. "Children of the night," Bela Lugosi would have mused in rapture at these eerie howls. "What music they make."

Taking my dogs hiking in the Catskills where an amazing network of trails awaited us was always an adventure. Fly was too unpredictable to go off-leash with the other dogs, but I never saw him happier than when he was running with my pack on a fifteen-foot lead through the deep woods. Spirits of ancient lupine ancestors awoke as we whisked through cool semidarkness thick with pure oxygen you couldn't get in the city, except maybe in oxygen bars, or in hospitals. Fly inhaled all his chest could hold and soldiered on like a champ, though his tiny, fragile body would have been meat to any wolf if he ever broke free to discover his family tree.

One Sunday morning on the way back to New York, I stopped at the sleepy welfare town's local diner called "The Robin Hood." I left the dogs in the rental car—not considered abusive at the time, if done responsibly—parked in the shade with the windows cracked, right up front to keep an eye on them from a window booth. My pancakes and sausages arrived when a woman stormed in from the parking lot, shouting hysterically that a small dog was inside a locked car screaming his head off and needing help. Of course she meant Fly, the dog who managed to get himself into snafus no matter where we went, who took years off my life in that year I homed him. I rushed outside, unlocked the car door, but saw no sign of him, just five dogs sitting well-behaved on the back seat. Reaching under the driver's seat, I felt a skinny leg and pulled.

Fly had managed to get himself stuck inside an old Lay's potato chip bag left by some other car renter centuries ago, a relic missed by generations of cleaning crews in some secret place only Fly, always off the beaten path in search of trouble, would find. Crumbs were involved. Once he was in and had scarfed down his fill, like Winnie the Pooh after he ate too much honey at Rabbit's house, Fly found he couldn't squeeze his way back out. A most ignoble end. The little guy in my hands wasn't moving and my heart sank. I tore off the snack-food shroud, sure this salty dog was dead, but suddenly his legs jerked and nostrils flared as he gasped wildly for air. His eyes opened wide in Vaudevillian surprise, a gag performed many times in nearby theater resorts of the olden days, and soon Fly was back to normal, for whatever that was worth. Relieved as I was he'd made it—I'd come to love the tyke terror despite all the trauma he'd caused me—another near-tragedy meant the fostering had to stop. Two days in the country, and my nerves were shot.

A month later, after interviews with candidates forewarned of his pedigree peculiarities and still willing to take him on because they wanted a Min Pin—don't ask me why—Fly was happily set up with an eccentric elderly gentleman who lived in a huge mansion in rural Connecticut. There, Fly could do all the damage he wanted. Outdoors, he had formal gardens to dig up as desired. Indoors, he had forests of carved Victorian furniture legs to gnaw on and mark, legions of servants to clean his messes from priceless antique carpets, to poach him organic chicken breasts in dry white wine with steamed asparagus tips. The little shit. I wanted that job. Fly had freedom to do what he pleased on the estate. He even chased a local farmer down the dirt road one day, I'm told.

Long after Fly was rehomed, I kept returning to that idyllic place where my dogs and I ran off-leash for hours, splashing in streams and waterfalls and forgetting all about the city. Sadly, the Borscht Belt began an uncertain comeback as a destination spot and the seedy motel was sold and torn down to make way for something fancier. Prices soared, and they stopped allowing dogs. But for years until our dream vacation was over, I and mine spent weekends wandering endless trails over mountainsides and beyond, so lost in our freedom that we sometimes forgot to turn around early enough to get back to the car before dark.

That oxygen was what kept us going. In fact, after the World Trade Center fell and while it sat smoldering for months, I was busy working, and a bit shell-shocked from the attacks, and made the mistake of not getting out of the city with my dogs. On days when the wind was right, my apartment filled with the smoke of burned bodies, or worse, and from my window I saw figures rushing along hazy streets, faces covered with scarves that made them look like terrorists.

We all became sluggish, depressed, and paranoid. Starting to sense how much this bad atmosphere was affecting me, and my dogs, I finally headed back to the mountains with six or eight friends overcrowding the back seat of another rental car. The dogs unloaded themselves as though catapulted by springs, and the moment we hit that trail I felt a surge of energy that made me dizzy and made the dogs go wild. It was the oxygen.

Hiking with a pack of dogs can be a path to self-discovery. I don't think I'm overreaching by speculating that when we're moving confidently and gracefully in unison along an ancient path in the deep woods, something primal kicks in, for both me and my dogs. The feeling is overwhelming and hard to describe, and maybe can't be accurately, but has something to do with movement and position relative to each other. A sense of well-being comes over me, and my little legion, the kind of contentment that comes with being in a place and time with no desire to be in any others because all is as it should be. I'm a firm believer, after many such outings, in the theory that prehistoric hominids first befriended wolves, not around villages where some say garbage heaps attracted them, but on the great hunting highways where we learned from each other—us more from them, I suspect—long before humans became sedentary and wolves became dogs.

Running free, of course, isn't all fun and games. The wild is no amusement park. I've never lost a dog in town or country, but some of my clients have let their loved ones dart off after a rabbit or a deer, never to be seen again. Those poor creatures likely starved to death, or froze. Others may have met predators, perhaps some old relations.

I believe my pampered big-city canines have gained as much self-knowledge on the trail as I have. More often than not, never having been taught or told, they simply know what to do to run as a pack. Happily out of their urban "heel" positions, they fall naturally into line along a path. Some may have never been to a city park, much less to the wide open country, and still they tend to understand this is no free-for-all being off-leash in the wild. Certain dogs, like my own sweet Samantha, instantly assume the scouting position, up front a few yards from the rest of us, while others flank us on both sides, off the path and out in the underbrush. Some tag along as rear guards not far behind. Fraidy-cat humans, scared of their own shadows and better off back in town, are always whining about free-ranging canines they encounter on their bird-watching expeditions. They complain to park rangers that we're threatening "the environment," and them. If they stopped being such whiners for a minute and watched closely, they'd see how orderly my canine congregation is. For the most part, barring some tempting scent, my dogs stay on the straight and narrow, and to their positions, and they wouldn't hurt a fly, or a butterfly collector. No commands are needed, as I suspect my ancestors didn't need spoken language to work with wolves, a trait as overestimated, again, as my opposable thumbs holding a hiking stick I picked up along the way.

Sounds far-fetched? Something taught my dogs to assume their positions and I assure you it wasn't me. It's possible, I'll admit, that walking as a team on city sidewalks helped prepare them for off-leash outings—and it can't hurt to keep liver treats in my pockets on the trail, just in case—but this doesn't explain everything. I've hiked with every shape, size, color and combination of greyhound, shepherd, beagle and mutt to assume a position, and unless a retriever's irretrievably inbred and not too swift in either town or country, he'll be trusted free-ranging and fall right in line. Just about any dog can do it.

One of the most rewarding sights in all my years of taking clients' dogs hiking was that of a tiny lapdog, of the white-and-fluffy genus, a type you'd never expect to see in a woodland setting, lighting up on his path to self-discovery. The small Shih Tzu named Ryan, stylin' with a puppy cut to ward off the burrs and discourage ticks from hitching a ride, kept up like a trooper for miles, leaping over fallen trees, diving into streams, tackling steep rock inclines, overjoyed to finally learn what it's like to be a dog.

CHAPTER FOUR

Back in town, after an orgy of territorial pissing on lush mountainsides each has claimed as his or her own, my dogs resign themselves to peeing on pavement already reeking with counterclaims. For me, it's back to the daily drudgery of dealing with other humans and fending off their sometimes inane and irritating questions.

I have reasons to suspect that when tourists stop me for help, they're often as interested in chatting me up about my furry friends, perhaps petting and even talking to them, not me, as taking down directions. Dogs are a familiar comfort, down-to-earth and homey whether you're from Japan, France or Michigan. Their uncanny ability to put smiles on wary faces brings people together in unplanned ways. Dogs blast us back to a moment in childhood, maybe to that first puppy found under a Christmas tree, or the wish never come true but still so badly missed.

Drawn by the prospect of puppy love and eager to make it last, strangers gear up to ask that second question, the one I'm almost guaranteed to get, just after where to find that fabled "village" they're already in.

"What breed is this one?" they ask of whatever latest trendy dog *du jour* I've been hired to promenade for everyone's enjoyment.

Tourists, like many locals who still don't know better, soon learn they're barking up the wrong family tree. Here's where I stop being informative and start getting downright preachy. They all know very well what breed this one is, and the others as well. They just want to dazzle me with their acumen, to hear me speak the magic words they've heard on television once every year when the Westminster show is aired live from Madison Square Garden a few blocks away. "Jack Russell," "black Lab," and "Cavalier" are self-affirmations that not everything about New York is too sophisticated for them, that they're not as provincial as they've been made to feel. My mission, should I choose to accept it, is to make a case for true curiosity, not dreary clichés, to appeal to their natural sense of adventure by steering them away from the cookie-cutter brands like Samsung, Adidas, and golden retriever they should have left in their hotel rooms in Times Square, or back home when they supposedly set out to experience things new and different. Like a dog trainer with treats, I lure them from their prefab profiling with tales of another beast, the real-life individual dog with his or her own unique merits that have nothing to do with standard coat color, family background, or starring roles in major motion pictures. My mission is to awaken them to all those endearing details and quirks, not flaws, that make up a dog's "personality," for lack of a better word, to guide them beyond this silly business of breedery.

Since I got into this line of work twenty years ago, it's been an honor and privilege to promenade every style of canine flesh and fur that's been fashionable—and then to shed my prejudices about this breed or that once I meet the real dog underneath. I've known most of my friends since they were wee pups, and I arrived daily to free them from their training-crate solitude. Long before they even started looking like the breeds their owners saw in advertisements, I plopped these tiny fuzz balls down gently on pages of *The New York Times* spread across the kitchen floor for their edification. By the time they're old enough to save their commentary for the sidewalk, and fast enough to keep up with my pack, I've grown more attached to them than I am to my multiple leashes.

In fact I'd know my dogs only by their names, not their breed names, were it not for the hordes of name-droppers on the pavement constantly reminding me what new buzzword I'm escorting.

A good buddy of mine named Percy, who just happens to be what society calls a black Labrador retriever, has been trying his whole life to live down his elitist past, and his coat color, and get down to playing fetch in the local dog-run dirt. He's not interested when fans block our path and bow as if to royalty, forcing us into stop-and-chats on how fine a race his is. Percy, who has places to go and things to do, turns up his nose and actually tries to get around them.

"Not to be rude," I try to explain, "but he has a busy schedule." Fans are not amused, but do have another story of those nasty New Yorkers for the folks back home.

Gilda, a golden girl of my acquaintance, would rather not ride on the reputation of dead relations, but sits without being told in the hope that strangers will have cookies. That's really all she wants from them, not praise for her credentials.

Herbie the Yorkie looks as sweet as pie. Just don't let him too close to your face.

Pinkie the pit isn't even a breed, and still she gets called names.

"How old is he or she?" many inquiring minds ask, skipping the breed question and going straight to age and gender. "Don't be ageist, and stop imposing binary pronouns," is my standard reply.

Sometimes these connoisseur kitties get too curious for their own good. Driven by their quest for trivia, they force me to be obnoxious.

"Why yes, he's a Komondor, and a perfect specimen," I answer. "He has the precise number of curls the AKC allows. Wanna count them?" Not a crowd-pleaser, my sarcasm can be smelled from a mile away by the least sophisticated pedestrians.

"What a rude man you are!" more than one slighted stranger has spat when passed without a word of validation.

Everywhere we try to go, my dogs and I, and whether it's the visitors or the locals giving us the hardest time, there's this almost universal assumption that we're out solely for the public's enjoyment, that dogs are put on this planet only to alleviate someone's boredom and boost the latest craze, beliefs that have caused more trouble for dogs than I dare discuss here. People think they're being clever standing out from the crowd with their interesting questions, but if they had any idea how many people just like them pursue us, and with the exact same insightful queries and educated guesses, they might stop to think before trying to make us stop and waste our time, and making my job more difficult than it already is. Anyone who thinks I'm rude should go ahead and try being out here on the sidewalk for hours on end, hit with the same lame requests hundreds of times each day, year after year, when my purpose is to give these dogs some exercise, to let them relieve themselves, and get them to the park to play before their paid time runs out.

If I do decide to engage over matters canine, it's not for anyone's free entertainment. If I'm waiting for a light to change and have nothing better to do, sometimes I even have fun with my persecutors.

A favorite gag of mine, to tell them, straight-faced and authoritatively, that the obvious purebred before them, something you couldn't miss, like a Dalmatian, is "just a mutt," is guaranteed to leave them with a puzzled look. Or I'll invent breed names from thin air—I might as well make it worth my bother if they insist—throwing them off the scent, and hopefully helping them see how silly they're being.

"*Mais non*, I'm afraid he's not an Anatolian shepherd dog," one woman is devastated to learn. "That was a good try, but he's a very rare Egyptian Pencil Hound, and a perfect specimen at that." Another confused look, then a nod of agreement, as if to say: "But of course!"

"You're close but not on the money," begins another stupid pet trick of mine. "This most assuredly is *not* a Nova Scotia Duck Tolling Retriever, but a fine example of South American Filibuster." Some inquisitors are still unconvinced: "Just look at the subtle slope to the ears," I add expertly, "the almond-shaped eyes, the perfect symmetry of the markings, not to mention that regal stance." Inquiring minds agree, and no doubt apply my misinformation to any poodles they pass.

Dogs, it's true, can be used to bring people together, but they can also be used to push us apart. Rightful owners of this breed or that appreciate, better than anyone but me, what I'm up against. They, too, are relentlessly hounded day and night for having bitten off more than they can chew, socially speaking, and they pay me handsomely for my evasive techniques, however antisocial I must be when walking their dogs.

People can actually become violent when fawning over other people's pets. One woman I worked for bought a so-called "Tibetan terrier"—I know him simply as Ted—when that was all the rage. After she was chased down the street and called a "bitch" one morning on a hurried walk before work, by another well-dressed businesswoman who nearly tore her arm off for not dropping everything to discuss the pros and cons of her brand of choice, she swore never to buy a breed again, though she loved her Teddy. Unrequited puppy love can be toxic, and total strangers take it very personally, almost foaming at the mouth, if not acknowledged and indulged for as long as they demand.

Just recently, I myself had a run-in, this time with a very plump woman who was miffed when I didn't let her pet a border terrier I was walking—the twelfth person to ask in the previous half hour. It was a Friday night and the end of a very hard week. I was on the phone while walking and made a polite wave that said "That's alright. Not just now." The situation escalated quickly. She called me an "asshole." I told her to fuck off. She said I could just do something inappropriate for her. I called her something that can't be repeated here. The Chinese woman taking my dinner order on the phone was silent for a moment, then said: "You made a curse." The determined dog lover said I had no idea with whom I was dealing and that she would "send some guys to beat you up." It turned out the woman was connected, and the next day a very creepy character, a large man who could have been a cast member on *The Sopranos*, showed up in a black van at the very same spot to scare me, or perhaps to ID me. I filed two harassment complaints at the Sixth Precinct and the cops told me they knew exactly who these people were. They were known criminals and dangerous, and I should call 911 immediately if ever they came near me again. So far, I'm alright, but I'm no closer to giving in to strangers' demands to pet my dogs, border terriers or not.

Most people have no idea how crazy "dog lovers" can get when we try to pass, and how difficult doing my job—walk my clients' dogs, not do stop-and-chats with murderous psychopaths gluttonous for gooey affection—can sometimes be. A nice gay couple I work for understand exactly what I'm up against. They came close to actually giving up their new puppy, a Weimaraner, but had asked for everything they got when they bought such a high-profile breed. Pursued mercilessly wherever trying to take their little grey puparazzi magnet to pee, they found it practically impossible to walk poor Stella at all. Simply being seen with her in public drew crowds rushing at them, waving arms and speaking in baby talk. People lose all sense of civility, and self-control, when a skinny Weimaraner pup comes within their radar. I should know, having walked a few. Their huge paws clunking and long cartoon ears bouncing, these ambulant clinics offer free doses of cuddle hormones to total strangers starved for puppy love and out of their minds if they don't get fixes right then and there.

Having had her for only a few weeks, Stella's dads were exhausted and understandably paranoid. It was all their own fault for choosing a breed to impress and entice people, but I still felt sorry for them. These poor guys had been stalked and traumatized, made afraid to step outside with their own dog. One day they asked me about finding young Stella some other parents, perhaps in the country where she would have more room to roam and fewer fans to admire her coat. In a moment of desperation, they considered dyeing her to look like a dog of a different color, so distraught they'd been made by the hordes of dog lovers mobbing them to show how much they cared, to demonstrate what fine human beings they were simply for saying they loved dogs, not helping with the already difficult task of raising one in the city.

I convinced Stella's dads to hold on a few more months, just until she stopped looking like a puppy. Sure enough, by the time she turned a year old, most of those fervent dog lovers on the sidewalk had lost interest. They come back like a plague whenever someone else in my neighborhood gets a new Weimie pup for me to walk, these sophisticated aficionados of every shade of grey, with William Wegman to blame.

CHAPTER FIVE

Each dog is an individual, but because I love dogs, I don't think all types belong here.

Call me a breed basher on this Isle of Misfit Breeds, but why any human in its right mind would bring a hardwired hunting dog into the city is beyond me. I know, it's about looking sporty and aristocratic, or just drawing attention with something completely out of place, but if I didn't need cash from the proud owners of these inappropriate pets, I'd be asking them: Who's smarter—you or the dog?

Not many animals are half as nuts living in the city as the typical Weimaraner, a round peg of a dog people try to fit into a square hole of a tiny but ridiculously expensive New York apartment. And then they wonder what went wrong. Whether from a lack of information, social pretension, blind conformity—or all of the above—the impulse purchase of a Weimie is a formula for trouble. Most any dog by this name is a high-energy, tightly wound, testy type, tougher to manage than most can handle, and hard to keep happy in a place where providing enough exercise is next to impossible. When an unknown artist in the seventies made goofy home movies with his dogs for *Saturday Night Live*, then made a fortune taking silly pictures of them dressed as humans, he must have known what a senseless fad he was starting.

One animal of this ilk I walked for a couple years was that stressed-out specimen named Stella. This girl's two fashionable Chelsea dads were chronically style-conscious and had quite an eye for the latest accessories. Conspicuously displayed on their coffee table was a book of photos by the aforementioned artist. They kept their elegant blue-grey dog in a cramped but ultramodern Chelsea one bedroom where she sat waiting each day for me to take her down the sidewalk runway for passersby to admire. Her dads were in the fashion industry but poor Stella could never seem to find enough work. The city's dog parks weren't big enough for her to move as she'd been designed. Letting her free-range in Central Park, even during the legal off-leash hours, was not an option because she was too easily seduced by birds and squirrels and likely not to return. Over time, hyperactive, underactive Stella grew, not easier to handle, but crazier and less manageable. On sidewalks she was constantly attacking other dogs, and her dads came to think of it as normal to have several lawsuits running simultaneously. I kept a firm grip on her at all times—until I got a hernia, had surgery, and was out of work for several months with nerve damage that has lasted to the present day.

Up until my injury here on this Isle of Misfit Breeds, I did my best to help Stella have fun in the short periods I had her. The more I tried, though, the clearer it was she probably shouldn't have been in the city at all. Her owners, rather than choose a less active breed with less demanding needs—or better yet, rescue a local dog regardless of coat color, one already here and needing a home—went to superhuman lengths to make everything else fit *her*. Each day at the end of Stella's disappointing half-hour outing in a miniscule, paved, enclosed area in the middle of a highway cloaked in car exhaust and called a "dog run," I returned her to her ultramodern Chelsea apartment that was painstakingly composed as though to accommodate an animal who needed desperately to belong—or maybe the dog was chosen to go with the digs, in which case Stella blended in perfectly.

A strictly disciplined composition of black, white, and various shades of grey was this animal's unnatural habitat, the only milieu she'd ever known. No other colors could be found in this place, and I searched high and low. Stella lived and lounged amidst sleek, low-backed grey leather sofas from Italy with big, shaggy, cream-colored pillows. She had silver chrome tables and chairs set against stark eggshell walls, and jet-black kitchen appliances and stereo equipment offset by bright white Apple computers. Her dads had an art collection, beautiful to behold, but doggedly limited to the likes of charcoal figure drawings on pearly backgrounds, black Japan ink paintings on rice paper scrolls, muddy grey watercolors of approaching storms. There were signed-and-numbered

Helmut Newton photos from the seventies depicting, in silver nitrate tones, long and leggy people with striking sinewy bodies uncannily like Stella's own. (In order to show off a stunning sculptural musculature, Weimaraners were robbed, through unnatural selection, of an undercoat needed by any dog to keep warm in winter.) No hues beyond the black-to-white spectrum were allowed in her carefully controlled environment, or on shivering Stella herself, on her collar, leash, harness, sweater, raincoat, bowls, balls or chewy toys, all selected in various shades of grey to approximate her own.

One afternoon, at the end of a tension-packed walk and a frustrating visit to the Chelsea "dog run," I was about to leave Stella alone in her matching décor and get on with my busy day in the garish world outside. I placed a handmade organic black designer dog biscuit squarely on her favorite contrasting surface, an ivory alpaca shag rug between the grey leather sofa and the silver chrome coffee table. I slowly turned the silver aluminum Philippe Starck door handle and opened the mirrored front door to exit, then turned around, as I did for all my dogs, to check one last time that everything was alright before leaving.

Where the hell was Stella? Not five seconds earlier, I'd left her right there on a contrasting rug, and she was nowhere in sight. Blood pressure rising, I searched the kitchen, bedroom, bath and beyond, but couldn't for the life of me spot her in this "Find the Stella" picture. Desperately seeking Stella, and unwilling to believe she could just vanish, I returned to the living room and stared my hardest at a landscape with which she'd merged imperceptibly.

Her black organic designer dog biscuit all finished, this wacky Weimaraner had jumped up on the sofa where she blended so well that I honestly couldn't see the canine for the cushions—until one of them moved when I called out her name.

Caring for other people's pets, I myself sometimes get lost in the scenery and need to step back for perspective. Despite all the decorating demands, Stella was truly loved by her man-parents, who when it came down to it probably had similar stylistic concerns for any relationship they wanted to sustain, including their own. Apart from the obvious emotional needs dogs fill for their humans, it's these many *other* strange uses people find for them, how they're shaped into tools for the most specialized tasks—like matching the furniture, impressing people with the latest fashions, or living up to impossible breed standards set by someone long ago for reasons no one can remember—that fascinate me no end.

Based on my ample experience with consumers and their catalog canines, in private and revealing settings the public seldom sees, I can say that while the first attraction to a particular breed is usually based on something as superficial as the coat—favorite colors or dazzling markings, bogus hypoallergenic claims, whether a shedder's hair will show on the furniture—once all but the coldest-hearted souls get their standardized items home, they fall in love and bond for life with the *individuals* under all that packaging—only to backtrack and believe it was by sticking to cosmetic breed standards that they found the perfect pets to match their personalities and lifestyles!

Assuming, of course, that theirs are as special and unique as they imagine their superficially-diverse breeds to be. What to make of these nostalgic claims to "form and function" in house pets today? Do they really need to look the ways they do just to find places in our hearts and homes?

Still stuck on coats, I once knew a brown cocker spaniel named Irving who gave new meaning to the term "working dog." Energetic and always in need of a job, Irving was an ambassador for a breed that, transformed into an inbred, over-combed monstrosity for show rings and front parlors, had drifted far from its true ancestral calling. Pet cockers haven't been bred for hunting skills in generations, neurotic though they are from inheriting some of the old temperament. Bizarrely shaped by doggy hairdressers to match the illustrations on the AKC's website, Irving's type no longer even resembles the original models, some of which can still be seen sweeping the fields of an English countryside for birds called woodcock. Men who actually hunt with dogs laugh at the blown out curly hair extensions on the ears of redux cockers like Irving the house pet. They roll their eyes at the elaborately long and decorative fringe hanging off his underbelly, the great bell-bottom trousers that deform his legs and make this pathetic poof of a pup look something like a Southern debutante in an enormous hoop skirt. Fancy frills rule out running over hills for birds without tripping in the underbrush. If not ensnared and crying for help in those curly locks, cockers bred for purely pet purposes would come back loaded with grass, burrs, twigs, leaves—everything but the bird.

Irving bore scant family resemblance to distant relations who gave him, and his owner, their airs of aristocracy. He'd inherited none of the talents that made these dogs so helpful to have around the estate—or had he?

One day I witnessed the clever new way Irving's mom had found for him to earn his keep, a bizarre new twist to the "form and function" thing. As it turned out, that fruity fringe on this dog's underbelly, purely ornamental with no utilitarian end in view, actually made him useful. Irving's mom kept a very clean house, and while her maid tried to keep the floors spotless, getting a vacuum cleaner under the huge canopied bed in the guest room seemed a lost cause. The combined strength of the two women failed to move the bed, and short of calling a maintenance man, or me, every week to help sweep, nothing could be done. That was when Irving, the hunter-turned-lapdog, came running to the rescue.

Had I not seen it, I never would have believed. My client, Irving's mom, tossed a tennis ball under the bed, and her half-cocked cocker burrowed eagerly under to retrieve. Seconds later, he emerged with the ball in his mouth, tail wagging, a proud look on his face—and dust bunnies suckling on his befringed belly. Irving's mom tossed again, then again, and again, each time the maid and I laughing, and Irving loaded with more dust bunnies, until the floor under the bed was clean, and the dog needed to be vacuumed.

Not all uses people find for the dogs in my life are as practical as housecleaning. "More about people than dogs" barely scratches the surface for intricate tasks these animals perform, for what people think they're doing for them but are really doing for themselves. Over the years, I've been a paid accomplice to some very strange employments of our four-footed friends. Once I agreed to take on a red Siberian husky named Pushkin, owned by a philosophy professor at NYU, a born-and-bred American. I had to invest in Rosetta Stone CDs so I could walk his dog in Russian.

Another time I boarded, and raised on my own, a gentle and lovable Bernese mountain dog named Reginald, from puppyhood to the age of three while his neurotic heiress mom roamed the earth for the right spa to cure her long list of imaginary allergies. More than once I was tempted to lighten Reggie's burden since birth, the heavy coat that's a major attraction on the breed, and have the poor fellow shaved in the dog days of August. His mom would have been furious to see him no longer looking like the pictures on the AKC's website, though she seldom saw him at all. Independent of practical considerations like comfort—or whether you ever managed to see your own dog—it was becoming very fashionable at the time to import exotic creatures meant to be farm dogs in the cool Swiss Alps, forcing them to endure the stifling heat, the horrid humidity, and the scorching pavements of summertime Manhattan. How my Reggie boy did suffer to wear the coat his mom so fancied, though she was seldom there to see it.

Included in my pay during those three years of raising Reginald was an allowance for riding my bike to the city's first Whole Foods store in Chelsea—"Whole Paycheck" was the joke back then—and return, backpack loaded with wild buffalo burgers and ostrich steaks costing twenty dollars per doggy dinner. These were all this pup's hypochondriac, made-of-money mom was convinced Reggie's own fictional allergies would permit.

I had high hopes that my client would one day find a place to live that would agree with both her own fictional allergies and her dog's desperate need for a cooler climate. Sadly for Reggie, he met his mom down in Texas to spend the rest of his life in an even more oppressive atmosphere for a dog bred to live in the Swiss Alps.

I've also had the (mixed) pleasure of knowing an endearing but miserable purebred boxer named Sadie. Her young dad bought her because he was a history buff and liked the idea of having a famous war dog breed from another era. Unlike Reginald the Bernese whose owner's imaginary afflictions were projected on him, Sadie really did have allergies and the symptoms were quite devastating. Results, these were, of a history of inbreeding to keep her blood "pure"—the boxer was the breed chosen by scientists to first map the dog genome because it was so inbred and genetically simple—and despite her historically-accurate coat from birth, Sadie never could quite live up to her dad's dream of owning a nostalgia breed. So badly did Sadie's skin itch, she literally chewed it off on a daily basis. By the age of two, her coat was a bloody, war-torn patchwork of open sores and scars, little left of the stately "mahogany," or the dramatic white "flashes" given points by judges in the ring. Dashing her dad's expectations, Sadie didn't look at all like those boxer illustrations on the AKC's website. He did love her, though.

A special diet gave Sadie some relief from her allergies, but only eased her agony. Whenever her dad travelled, I enjoyed her sweet company and tended to her fragile health, keeping the vet's phone number emblazoned upon my brain, and feeding her the only food on the planet that seemed to help a bit. If we ran out, Dad's credit card in hand, I dialed a limousine service that brought me to the Upper East Side—and the Eastern Seaboard's exclusive purveyor of kangaroo kibble.

There's nothing some people won't do for their dogs. If I blame them for paying breeders to go on producing troubled animals, I respect them for seeing their beloved friends through to the bitter end. But if they go out and buy into the same cycle of cruelty again, they just might find themselves in my next book.

CHAPTER SIX

When I decided to migrate to New York from suburban Michigan in the early eighties, I braced myself for those "rude New Yorkers" I'd heard so much about. I also prepared to confront the "dangerous" city so feared by my fellow provincials, most of them never having so much as seen the place, and forgetting the fact that nearby Detroit, my birthplace which few bothered visiting, actually outranked New York as murder capital of the world.

As usual, myth overrode reality in public opinion. A year before I landed on Manhattan, a film called *Escape from New York* was in theaters across the country, and here I was, eccentric or mad, everyone thought, to be moving in the opposite direction.

Suspecting that much of the front-porch gossip about big, bad Gotham simply wasn't true, I was, admittedly, mugged twice in my first year here, but soon grew street-smart and stopped acting like a dumb tourist. Learning the lay of the land, I felt, and was, safer even in New York's most sordid spots than in those vast deserted spaces of the bombed-out metropolis where I was born. This was because there were always so many people around. Living for several years just off Times Square, pre-Disney and still very much Diane Arbus, a congested neighborhood famous and infamous for prostitution, drugs, and severed heads found in hotel rooms, I found that crossing the sleazy 42nd Street freak show, counter-intuitively, was the safest way to get home at night. Tourists from back home gaped and pointed at me, one of the freaks now, through closed windows of taxicabs—the old Checker cabs made in Kalamazoo, Michigan, where I went to grade school—tiptoeing past cowardly with doors locked.

New York's rowdy crowdedness, oddly enough, is not only the source of its safeness and allure, but the ultimate reason for visitors, those with the courage to exit their cabs, taking home their prized war stories of those "rude New York-ers" who mistreated them in some way—then coming back the next year for more abuse. Poor them, who stepped bravely into the maelstrom, only to be roughly squeezed past, sum-marily bumped, dismissively scolded for being in someone's way. Worse yet: ignored and invalidated by the scores of total strangers. Millions get bypassed without so much as a neigh-borly smile or an engaging conversation on the weather or the dogs I'm walking. Rather than accept an honest cultural difference, and a New Yorker's pressing need to get from point A to point B with minimal obstruction, they interpret each random antisocial encounter as some sort of personal slight directed intentionally at them—and they say New Yorkers have big egos!

Like the time one of my visiting in-laws got all huffy over being accidentally brushed in a tiny Village restaurant on Cornelia Street where there's barely enough room to hold a fork, much less to manspread.

This is not to say that living here is all smooth and easy, that New Yorkers aren't pissed off regularly by other New Yorkers, just that survival in a foreign culture is a learning process. If I cut my streetwise teeth landing on this edgy, overbuilt piece of rock, then I earned my PhD in crowd management working here as a full-time dog walker. Imagine, if you can, the extra layer of complexity that's added to the whole New York riddle of how to get from point A to point B without killing someone—when I monopolize much of the concrete *with a pack of dogs.*

Right up there with tourists and bicyclists as a nuisance in the minds of many, I can't help but fan my web of leashes across the same sidewalk claimed by hordes trying to get to work on time, brats flying by on scooters with my dogs nipping at their heels, zombies ignoring their steps and stepping on paws while texting something that apparently can't wait. Who gets to pass and who moves aside, who must be tripped by my leashes and who should apologize, is not an easy legal matter of right-of-way, not like cars crossing intersections or making left turns. As happens with that purely symbolic jaywalking law flaunted universally by New Yorkers, to the horror of naïve visitors from more orderly places, the cops, as a practical matter, turn a blind eye to pedestrian squabbles, turning us over to the law of take-your-own-chances and every-man-and-dog-for-himself.

What, if any, are my rights-of-way as a dog walker in a concrete jungle where pretty much anything goes? Not only are the rules vague, but my days are spent in constant negotiation of social contracts that are unwritten but continually *re*written depending on the general mood. I test the ground with each step forward, bushwhacking my dogs' way through a landscape thick with natives who aren't always hospitable. Most people we meet, these days, are dog lovers, and go out of their way to proclaim so because this is the thing to be, or maybe because they really mean it.

Still I lock horns with unfriendly types, those creeps who go out of their way to give us a hard time, exchanging a hostile fire of *fuck you*s with me as I pass. Some people legitimately are afraid of dogs. I tell them to grow up. Some just dislike anyone attached to them. I call them things that can't be printed here. Some just use us to vent frustration over something else, anonymously and with minimal cost, then float through the rest of their day with a smug and exhilarating sense of victory. I learned early on that blowing off steam at someone else's expense—like trolling on Twitter—is what an inexhaustible supply of total strangers is for in New York.

Obstacles are the exceptions, not the rule, for today's dog walker, and ritual confrontations over canines are rarer than ever. But it wasn't always this pleasant for someone holding a leash to get around town. I've heard the war stories from old-timers who took on the heroic task of walking dogs back in the turbulent seventies, just before I arrived. This was because dogs really were causing problems, as I've written in another book, about New York's famous "poop scoop" law.

More so than other cities, New York is an intensely pedestrian culture with a premium on space. Freeing walkways of pungent piles that brought human traffic to a slippery halt, and restoring some semblance of peace, wasn't so much thanks to the law itself. Litter laws, like traffic laws, are virtually unenforceable, as every litterer and speeder knows. The sidewalks were made cleaner, and dogs were made more socially acceptable, because consensus combined with social pressure decided this new custom—bending over and bagging the unspeakable—was a good and necessary thing to do. New York became the first large city in the world with a successful poop scoop law because it had no choice, having reached a critical impasse and needing some agreement on minimal duties toward fellow New Yorkers. Screw the tourists.

Gone are the days when vigilante mobs combusted spontaneously to chase pedestrians down sidewalks for the crime of being seen with four-legged pollutants (one eye on the pavement for landmines). Despite what a few neurotics still say today, basically all dog owners are now picking up after their own, and anyone who flies off the handle over a chance encounter with an isolated turd, as far as I'm concerned, doesn't belong here and should move to some pristine suburb, like the one I escaped. Sadly, all it takes is a few of these annoying perfectionists to take a slide and dial 311, registering their trauma and amplifying the public's perception of how much unclaimed poop there actually is. Politicians eager for issues, and a press hungry for headlines, jump on the bandwagon to scapegoat dogs and their "irresponsible owners" for all the city's ills.

Overlooking these cheap opportunists who make so much a-doo about nothing, it's uncanny how times have changed for me and my motley crew. No one could have possibly predicted, back in those angry seventies, how *very* socially acceptable, once an arms-length agreement was reached about poop-scooping, walking around with a dog on one's sleeve would become. In fact showing unconditional approval of all things canine has become, by and large, a minimal qualification for being a good New Yorker!

It's not unusual for me to be squeezing my furry throng down a narrow Village sidewalk, never designed for so many people or pets, would-be passersby overflowing off the curb and onto a street never meant to accommodate so many vehicles—or zombies standing in the middle of traffic texting what can't wait—and have pedestrians almost overeager to step aside and apologize to *me* and my friends for being in *our* way!

This happens most everywhere we try to go. I was wary of the kindness of total strangers when I first got into this line of work, but soon learned there's no sarcasm attached to these gestures. People are genuinely sorry for taking up space, and time, that might otherwise be used by my dogs, and state their solidarity with us in the most public way. Each day, as we head out to confront the Great World with all its snags and detours, more big smiles than nasty glares await. Cheerily letting us pass, I imagine our obliging hosts are thinking, is the least they could do for having their stressful days brightened by therapy pets whose presence sooths their inner savage beasts. Science tells us, after all, that dogs lower blood pressure, ward off heart attacks, and give people longer lives with more places to try to go. What's there not to be thankful for? In a few short decades, dogs have gone from being seen as public nuisances in New York, threats to our very health and safety, the cause of an abrasive civil war—to being lifesavers, peacemakers, the very social lubricants we need to avoid killing each other when trying to get from point A to point B.

"*Thank you!*" is all I can think to say to those kind souls offering to let us pass.

The warmer months tend to be less complicated for sidewalk travel. Winter, you might not think, is when things heat up on a New York thoroughfare. Tensions rise when a big snowstorm chokes an already overcrowded city. There is, it's true, that initial valium effect, that loss of ourselves in childlike romps under falling snow, dances around trees in parks and each other on pavements. A kind of giddiness sets in, and for a brief and magical moment New Yorkers step out of character. The whole town turns into a friendly little village, more like that village the tourists have in mind when asking how to find "the Village" they're already in. Total strangers smile as they pass, zany enough to say "Hi!" to their neighbors, who some-times turn out to be just visiting from Cincinnati. The least self-conscious among us drop to make snow angels, and not even Currier and Ives could render these scenes any quainter. A big white blanket softens the concrete jungle, cushioning the hard edginess of urban life, buffering us from each other. Enough snow, and pesky automobiles are no longer welcome. The streets are ours, and cops look the other way as dogs plow merrily and safely off-leash across a winter wonderland.

The morning after is the hangover from all that revel-ing. New Yorkers awake to face the same unforgiving sched-ules but must climb over virgin drifts to meet them, or glacial piles of packed snow pushed from streets onto sidewalks by dutiful plows, and getting along, especially with each other, becomes trickier. Across unshoveled stretches sometimes spanning entire blocks, the massive flow of human migra-tion etches razor-thin footpaths into snow that soon hardens, making these meandering one-laners—over routes of ancient indigenous trails, I like to imagine—the only way to go. If the temperature drops and it's too late to clear the mess, deep, narrow ice passages can constrict foot traffic for days, with fellow travelers balancing, slipping, falling, breaking limbs, and getting edgy.

It can be daunting at first to see a long line of people come at you on one of these impossible arteries, eyes frozen to gadgets for those texts that can't wait. This is a social situation no less tricky than running into another hiker on a skinny ledge thousands of feet up a cliff in the Grand Canyon, the Colorado River roaring far below, an encounter I've had more than once. Who will step aside and onto shaky ground? Who gets to stay on course? Who will have to back up and start all over again?

Temperatures rise and the mess gets messier. Drains clog on street corners, making intersections all but useless. Great lagoons of muddy, frigid slush have nowhere to go but into shoes and boots, further irritants to struggling pedestrians. The young and agile gear up for large leaps, while the elderly, out of their depth, tempt fate by wading in. I have more than just myself to worry about. I clutch my smallest dogs tightly in my arms so they don't drown or float away, sacrificing dry socks and letting the larger dogs do their best to drudge across. That Currier and Ives moment has passed. The bleak and blinding winter sun adds insult to injury by exposing the filth behind what, just yesterday, seemed so pure and good.

Snowstorm withdrawal is the acid test for any New Yorker's patience and politeness. Walking dogs through these conditions, even if all the people were to magically disappear, would still be a challenge. I soldier on with four or five pups at once, some marching behind me like troopers in single file, others dangling in my arms. "Gizmo," the white teacup poodle, gets strapped in a carrier across my chest, his tiny pinhead popping through my ski jacket, some embryonic alien emerging from inside me and melting hearts everywhere we go.

You'd think that after snowstorms, when the fight for time and space in New York grows more cutthroat than ever, the runoff of stress would be dumped on me and my dogs. But the good New Yorkers detach their gazes from gadgets and step aside into snowbanks smiling, saving for later those texts that apparently could wait—while the inevitable asshole, who can't abide delays or drifts, rolls his eyes or clucks her tongue, because we stand between them and where they imagine themselves to be. But even with the forces of nature and nastiness stacked against us, we have that same fervent pro-dog sentiment to cheer us on, those same apologetic souls saying how very sorry they are to *me* for being in *our* way.

Sadly for my dogs, despite so much public support from all but the shrews, new developments make it seem they just can't win. Having city surfaces clearer than ever in recent years, and in some places relatively contention-free, has in some ways been making the sidewalk, not more but less hospitable to dogs. New York's newfound ability to stay on top of winter debris can actually make my dogs' lives harder than ever.

The more efficient and squeaky-clean New York becomes in these times of obscene wealth, overdevelopment, and hollow prosperity, the more hostile the obstacle placed in my pups' path. Salt mania—the excessive dumping of massive quantities of chemical-laced rock salt onto pavements to keep them perpetually free of the slightest congelation—burns their poor paws, and in more merciless amounts each year. These days, all it takes is an outside chance of a freeze, and uniformed doormen from enormous new luxury complexes, and keepers of storefront boutiques that sell frivolous items to fill them, are dumping truckloads of the evil corrosive on city surfaces, monopolizing entire blocks with the new gluttony for convenience and overcautious litigiousness, and causing serious problems for dogs.

Salt can curb my dogs' movement. From front doors where I leash them, to the gates of off-leash dog runs, their only sanctuaries in a city with precious few accommodations, they're just expected to walk over hot coals. Anyone who doubts my friends' suffering from ice overkill should try walking barefoot across their apartment floor after their dog has just dragged home some salt. This stuff is no joke. It burns like hell. But what to do? Many dogs flatly refuse to wear protective booties, much less walk in them. Applying ointments to their paws prevents some of the pain, but doesn't repel the same antifreeze chemicals we put in car radiators from being tracked in and licked off, sometimes fatally.

Everywhere we try to go on encrusted winter pavements, agonized cries can be heard in the distance, making me and mine uneasy. Dealing with surplus salt is a big part of what I do to protect my wards. If pedestrians were right in the seventies to complain that dog dirt was literally pushing them off the sidewalk and into the gutter, my choices with salt include: not walking the dogs and telling their owners to put down newspapers during winter months; dragging the dogs over the coals and ignoring their howls; carrying as many of the smaller ones as I can, letting them down only to poop or pee; or walking them all off the curb and into the gutter, closer to roaring traffic but with less concentrated salt than the sidewalks.

But dogs must be walked in rain, snow, sleet or shine. So the moment one of my friends starts to scream, I spring into salt rescue mode. My own homespun method depends on having some amount of snow nearby, but when it works, it's a lifesaver.

My salt solution is simple. When dogs lift their paws and look up at me in pain, I pick up the small ones, or lead the larger, to the closest patch of white dust some shovel missed, or as a second choice, to the nearest mountain of greyish snow and dirt the plows have left behind. I plop my dogs down squarely. The snow melts into their poor paws. The heart-wrenching cries subside.

I can only do so much, but do what I must. When no suitable spots on the ground can be found for my friends' relief, the last resort is the first parked car topped with the medicinal white powder. I lift my poor screaming pups, large or petite, and plant them firmly onto hoods and roofs, ignoring any damage I might do to someone's precious paint job. Motown is far behind me now, and car concerns go out the window when my wards' well-being is in the balance.

To be honest, my disrespect for automobiles is a bit more complicated, however much I do need them as a last resort for helping hounds. Besides being a dog walker who knows how dangerous passing cars are to his crew, I'm also an avid cyclist who knows the perils of the road and who his natural enemies are. No doubt, after countless collisions and brushes with death, having been hurled over opening taxicab doors, cut off and run off more times than can be recalled, I've come to harbor some resentment for these fat-assed, fossil-fueled hoarders of space and robbers of clean air. Like that stray jerk who uses me and mine to vent spleen over something else, I've learned to make the most of local resources while getting from point A to point B in New York—taking a jab at a pet peeve along the way.

CHAPTER SEVEN

Like everyone who comes to live in New York from as far as Michigan or as near as New Jersey, I had to learn the ropes. But then so must my mutts learn the lay of the land if they're going to survive, and much of that depends on following my lead and doing as I say.

In fact the French term for a "good" dog is *sage*, or "wise." This isn't to say everything dogs do in a human world is in their own best interests, or that people can any more agree on what intelligence means for themselves than they can define it for other animals. Much of being good, for dogs, is a relative matter of being smart enough to learn how to manipulate us. But whether being bad could be absolutely bad *for* dogs, I know from experience, presents a moral dilemma that often eludes the canine mind—but then, how many humans can claim they're any smarter?

The city sidewalk, where I struggle day and night to shield my wards from evil influences they couldn't possibly fathom, has taught me the limits of human foresight. It's uncanny how the very spots we've taught our four-legged friends, since they were pups, to pee and poo for praise and treats—the curb, for one, then those earthy areas around trees—also offer the most opportunities for them to mess up and come nose-to-nose with real, even life-threatening dangers. WTF were we thinking?

I can never be sure, knowing my furbabies' taste for mischief, what draws them to life on the edge of the curb. Are they sniffing for that perfect spot to evacuate, or is this a mere pretense for loading up? Don't think for a moment that dogs don't exploit my ignorance every chance they get. Scraps of strange fruit they ought not sample, molding pizza crusts, rancid chicken wings and worse are waiting 'round every corner to be snatched, then wrestled by me from a growling omnivore's jaws. Tossed paper cups sticky with sweet soda, food-encrusted plastic knives and forks, beer bottle caps, used condoms, crack vials, waffle cones emptied of gelato and soaked in chemical sludge leaked from parked cars, mounds of glass ground by street-cleaning-truck brushes and mixed with garbage juice from nearby restaurants into a tempting purée— with so many places for tempting morsels to congregate, it's not easy protecting dogs from themselves.

Watching me watching them, a second eye on prospects ahead, my wise guys are constantly on the lookout for ways to be bad. At best, an item pilfered on the sly is a harmless freebie. But ingesting a shard of glass, a hunk of rotting carrion, a wad of tin foil, a sharp stick, or food a tad too rich for a tummy, can be serious. Until only a few decades ago, before those grandiose, gated yuppie gardens buffering trees and begging to be watered by my crew, it was not unusual in the Village to find fresh trays of cookies and Rice Krispies treats, entire apple pies still steaming, beef roasts and meatloaves, pizzas still in the boxes, multi-tiered tiramisu (fashionable for a time both in sidewalk cafés and on sidewalks), all carefully propped against trunks with hand-scrawled paper plates reading: "PLEASE TAKE ME. FREE." The dogs licked their chops and would have moved in for the kill if allowed, though I'm sure that hungry humans, not as naively trusting as dogs, stopped to think twice before accepting these anonymous offerings, sugary, savory, or unsavory and too good to be true.

Not counting the raw steaks laced with pins or poison planted by dog-hating sickos—this has happened more than once in my neighborhood—random seductions await even the best-trained pets, luring them from the right path into behavior they know very well I expect them to resist. Keeping dogs safe got harder as the gap between haves and have-nots grew wider, and I struggled to shield my friends from a cornucopia of gifts grown on trees or left by woodland fairies. Street-food banquets were not typically intended for my dogs, however strongly they disagreed, and despite the obstacle course they presented, I felt heartened by such signs of humanity.

I scoffed at those less selfless acts of charity from overcompensated yuppies arriving in droves since the eighties to "bring New York back." They've succeeded at making much

of the city uninhabitable to anyone earning less than six figures, and they've crowded out the tree offerings, fretting over
their enclosed plots of decorative greenery, posting signs di-
recting us to the nearest curb instead. Public gestures to the
Great Outdoors, these pretentious ivy patches and pathetic
pansies—for "sustainability," they say—enhance property values even further. As the rich get richer and streets grow more
scenic, rather than give something back humbly and quietly
with charming, homemade dishes and hokey, hand-scrawled,
unsigned signs, the yuppies make points of inserting, as
though in passing at church socials, asides about how they
donate their valuable time to labor, a few hours every third
Saturday, in soup kitchens to "help the homeless." Compared
to their self-serving, the uncredited tree buffets were blessings
in disguise.

My four-legged friends also found family-style portions
charming, for as long as they lasted in New York, and they
could scurry for them faster than I might turn my head to
check a traffic light. Mostly, my dogs walked compliantly by
my side, looking innocent and obedient in their perfect "heel"
positions. But unlike humans said to live by higher principles,
their only concern at the end of the day, and despite appearances to the contrary, was whether I was watching.

Dieter the Doberman nabbed one of the marshmallows
crowning a bowl of fruit Jell-O, or so I was told after the fact
by a passerby one morning when not yet fully awake.

Miltie the corgi mix quaffed a hot dog *sans* bun without chewing, and in the time it took me to check the time.

Corazón, the klepto Chihuahua, secured a spicy taco and suffered for it later.

Love my dogs though I do, and wanting to believe they'd never betray my trust, as any New York lawyer will tell you: If no one saw it, then it didn't happen.

Even off the street have I tried, not always successfully, to protect my friends from themselves. Dog sitting in the home of a reporter for the BBC one night, preparing dinner I made the mistake of believing his faithful fox terrier was unwilling, or unable, to snatch food off the kitchen counter when I went to answer the phone. I wasn't even across the room when the wiry little weasel made his approach, springing like a tick and landing squarely on polished granite that scratched under his claws—deep-throating a five-pound block of Munster cheese before my eyes! The rascal had a surprised but proud look on his scruffy face, like a cat who'd just swallowed a canary he'd been stalking for years. How would I explain this to his owner? The next day he was fine despite my dire predictions of diarrhea.

Doing a sleepover in another home, on lower Fifth, with a sneaky beagle and pit bull who worked together, I was foolish enough to leave a large bowl of spaghetti with meatballs unsecured on the dining room table and go to the kitchen for some salt. Shaker in hand, not twenty seconds later, I returned to do a double take and question my sanity. Where was my dinner? The bowl had been licked shiny-clean of all traces of evidence, an operation performed surgically by professionals. Not a drop of sauce was spilled, and in the bowl a spotless fork and spoon gleamed to perfection, precisely in the same crossed position I'd left them. These two were good.

My own dog, the *sage* mutt Samantha, was famous for her obedience, but also for her problem-solving skills. Eager to please and talented enough to perform tricks on national television, she knew how to work a situation when my back was turned. At first I couldn't tell which dog—surely not my perfect Sammy, but one of the five others I was pet sitting that night—had purloined a roasted chicken from the counter and inhaled it, meat, skin, bones, cartilage and string, in the half-minute it took to let my dinner guests through the door. Sitting in a line-up for questioning, tail wagging with five others to say "It wasn't me," Sam was betrayed by greasy paw prints, in just the right size, leading straight to her. Vomiting ensued a half hour later.

My Samantha never would have assayed such a stunt alone, but competition, and the chance to blend in with a crowd and communalize blame, makes dogs, like us, do things we normally don't. Back on the street, who could honestly expect a pack of salivating pooches not to lunge in unison for a wounded cheesecake lying helplessly under a tree, drenched in cherry sauce and begging to be eviscerated like a tethered goat? You seldom see juicy big-ticket items in the Village these days, which has not made my job any easier. At least before, I knew my enemies who announced themselves honorably. New York is a bit tidier now than it was decades ago, but with the more obvious attractions gone, dogs have turned their talents to subtler, more insidious evils they once sidetracked while bolting for the real goodies.

Small food is easier for dogs to detect than me. They smell before I see, and again, exploit my ignorance when sniffing for a spot to go, or sniffing for a snack. Walking long enough with nose pressed to the ground, even the dumbest dog is bound to land on something eventually. The fact that there's still more than enough crap, in smaller portions, on city surfaces to go around doesn't make dogs any less competitive with the next one I'm holding back. The best of friends will scrap over the tiniest scrap, tearing each other apart if allowed, for a cracked peanut M&M or a Gummy Bear coated in fuzz.

Humans being no more rational, I remember how dog-eat-dog my fellow walkers were when the yuppies first started raking in their dough and employment was aplenty. Rather than build for a future, my unforesightful peers misspent their good fortune on backbiting, spreading vicious rumors about each other, fighting for jobs in a seller's market when they could have relaxed and been friends. One-upmanship and ruined reputations surely helped the corporate dog-walking services that came later, with their insurance and bonding, to put us out of business, lowering prices for the yuppies and giving us something to fight over, after all.

I often wonder if dogs see even me as vying with them for something they might have, whether they even want it or not. "What a waste," they must think as I navigate them, all eyes on the prize, around a piece of Cracker Jack rolled in dirt—only to leave it there unclaimed on the pavement like a cruel joke. Or do they think I'm not too bright to have missed it?

Then there are those hardcore consumers, the co-prophages, or poop eaters. "Why is he so keen on collecting my personal business in a doggie bag for later?" they must wonder. "Does he know something I don't?" The stock market comes to mind. Uninteresting as trends in waste products are to me, some dogs will spin around, determined to get in on the ground floor, and go for their own before news of it can hit the street.

Grabbing things simply because others might is for the bottom-feeders. The supreme pleasure for status seekers is to have what others can't afford. They pass us by the thousands each day on sidewalks, these scavengers, faces glued to absurdly-overpriced bits of plastic, texting mindlessly and following like drones the latest developments—stepping into piles before I have a chance to scoop.

Which leads me to that consummate consumer, the perfect eating machine, a veritable Hoover: my feisty friend Hatty.

"Swallow now, pay later" is Hatty's philosophy of life, though I doubt she's ever drawn a connection between her bottomless pit and her owners' sky-high vet bills. In this dog's mind, for lack of a better term, the sidewalk is an all-you-can-eat Las Vegas buffet, and the only reason for being out at all, or being in for that matter, is to stuff the whole world inside herself.

Love her though I do, enough to eat her right up, Hatty couldn't care less what she devours, or whether or not I'm watching, turning our daily strolls into battles of brute pulling strength. Over the course of her illustrious scrounging career, numerous X-rays, operations, and pumpings have produced an array of incredible inedibles ranging from felt and rubber remnants of masticated tennis balls, to polyester entrails and squeak boxes from bellies of gutted toy animals. Costume jewelry, nuggets of tin foil, used tampons, Legos, hundred-dollar bills in a silver Tiffany money clip, dirty socks and rocks—some items get lodged in her intestines, nearly costing her life.

One emergency vet visit produced no fewer than five used condoms stuck in Hatty's digestive tract. "You need to be more careful with prophylactics," the vet advised the couple who were relieved that everything had come out right and Hatty was out of danger. "We don't use condoms," said the wife.

Hatty's parents are divorced now and share their dog on alternating weeks. I still walk her but from two different addresses.

The product of a broken home, Hatty's even brattier now. She's known as an "English Lab," a breed that only the well-off can afford to have purged regularly, a feature that has not detracted from her appeal. A modified, kennel club version of her distant working ancestors once bred for agility and accuracy in retrieving downed birds for their masters' mantels, Hatty seeks only to enlarge her own private collection, and she answers to no boss. A personal favorite of many people, she looks like a big, yellow smiley face welded to four dwarfed, Teletubby legs. Being an "English," she's closer to the ground than traditional Labs, convenient for sidewalk scarfing and adding notches to her collar. At the local dog run, she hoards as many tennis balls as she can cram, four or five sometimes, sending muffled growls to dogs who come too close. An answer to the city's litter problem, she sucks up newspapers, leaves and branches, and she makes New York's poop scoop law redundant. She does everything but exercise and socialize, why we built dog runs in the first place.

Labs, "English" or not, are super-powered suction devices that must be watched closely at all times. Trying to keep a positive attitude toward his sometimes difficult dog, Hatty's dad once dressed her as a vacuum cleaner, strapping her with a hose and attachments, for the Washington Square Dog Run Halloween Costume Contest. She won first prize. But OCD eating makes Labs obese, no laughing matter. One website devoted to singing the praises of the Labrador brand tries to find some intelligent design behind all this obsessive-compulsiveness by answering the age-old riddle: "Why do dogs eat dirt?" Lacking solid evidence, apologists for Lab naughtiness say it could be due to some "mineral deficiency," meaning these dogs know exactly what they're doing when emptying flower pots and sweeping the pavement. This theory would, in theory, also cover the shreds of tire rubber I brake to pull from Hatty's mouth before they become blockages, and downing everything in sight is believed, desperately I believe, to be a sign of some deeper intelligence we're only just beginning to fathom. Bad behavior, devout Labbists suggest, could be some elaborate "attention-seeking device," a tool these crafty canines invented to harvest the resource they crave most: input from us, positive or negative, or as their owners say, "all good."

Or maybe yellow English Labs are just mindless eating machines that don't give a rat's ass one way or the other. Holding off on hasty judgments, I must admit there seems to be a method to Hatty's madness. Taking her home one evening, I felt a familiar tug on the leash as she lunged for a ball of used Kleenex some sniveler had dropped on the front steps of a brownstone townhouse. Exhausted and in no mood after an hour of tug-of-war, I gave Hatty a pass and let her grab it, hoping against hope she'd realize the prize was nothing special and spit it out so we could call it a draw, and a day. Knowing my friend's large appetites and taste for the game, I pretended not to care as she stood there defiantly, barely chewing but clicking her tongue as though to savor some fine wine. A faraway look came over her, and I half-expected she'd start waxing poetic on the facial tissue's rare vintage and sub-lime qualities, a complex bouquet with lofty aromas and hints of mint and lanoline, a smooth texture, earthy undertones, and a rich, toasty finish with notes of mucus but very dry.

Instead of spitting, she swallowed, then looked around for another.

CHAPTER EIGHT

I walk that extra mile for my friends, getting to know their favorite things to do, the types of dogs they like or don't, their good and bad habits, their endearing quirks. I'm available day and night for any last-minute outings, and I know how to handle the neurotic personalities of some of the owners. Like I said, this is the first paying job I've ever taken seriously, but you'd think that after all the tender, loving care I've given, the patience shown and shit endured, getting paid for my services should not have to be another struggle.

When I do get paid, I'm a happy camper. In fact if you ever want to mug someone, hit a dog walker late on a Friday afternoon. A dog walker who hasn't any large friends for protection. By that time, any poop bag-toting gypsy with the mettle to have lasted in this crazy business for twenty years will have amassed an astounding wad of cash for the week's travails, a healthy stack of greenback to compensate for his bad knees and hunching back, and no social life because he's in demand and always on call.

The hard-earned loot he carries, be forewarned, may be peppered here and there with a few stray personal checks the

walker doesn't want. Precise amounts are crawled on custom-
ized notes adorned with Florida sunsets in pastel tones, pink
ribbons to show breast cancer awareness, cartoon panda bears,
photos of the clients' dogs when wee pups—or just generic
with nothing but the facts.

Payment by check, instead of good, hard cash, tends to
come from the most demanding of dog parents, those who expect service with a smile, perfect punctuality, and every minute of a contracted half-hour walk. Exacting signatories put
their doormen on alert, and webcams on their home-alone
pups, in case I should try and rob them of any promised time.
Almost without fail, it's these same officious types, who want
everything done by the book—wouldn't you know it?—who
conveniently forget to stop by the bank on Thursday, then forget to leave any style of personal check on Friday, forcing me
to keep accounts.

Will I take PayPal? Perhaps Bitcoin? Don't get me
wrong. Most of my clients over the last two decades have been
as sweet as pie, generous at Christmas time, remembering I
have rent and health insurance to cover year-round whether
or not they pay me for the pleasure of their dogs' company.
They understand, without any begging, that I don't get paid
sick days (though a few kind souls insist on paying even when
I can't work), that vacation isn't included in my job descrip-
tion (though some actually give me spending money, so long
as I promise to come back). These relationships are about so

much more than business. Once people get to know and trust me, and see how much I really care about their dogs, we become friends. So personal is this personalized service I provide them, it can be a bit embarrassing to take their money at all. Still I hope they don't make me ask.

I have to be a hard-ass with some clients. The worst of them try to haggle with the help, or miscount the money left in an envelope on Friday enough times that it's no mistake. People take advantage, and while I might fall in love with their dogs, them I keep at a safe distance—until I have no choice but to fire them.

Like the guy with the two matching cairn terriers (the breed from *The Wizard of Oz*) who was at my place negotiating how boarding would work. I agreed to a two-for-one arrangement, as I do for smaller dogs when the owners are crying poorhouse (as he was), or when the dogs are rescued (which these two weren't). My price, including door-to-door service and more personal care than any commercial kennel for a much lower rate, was still too rich for this guy's blood, or so he said. Maybe I could throw in something else?

Now, I don't go tweeting #MeToo if advancement is offered in exchange for a roll in the hay, so long as it's with someone I'd want to roll with anyway (which this potential client wasn't). More than one down-low doorman has made it clear that helping a guy out couldn't hurt my business in his building. Unless he's ugly, I don't report him, or go acting all appalled to suddenly learn such injustices go on in this cold, cruel world. I gave no reply when the cairns' dad offered business for pleasure, but he seemed to know a good deal when he saw one and decided to "use" me just the same. Could I come pick up the boys at his place a week from next Sunday?

The two terriers whose dad had no money turned out to live on one of the best streets in the Village, in one of the most opulent buildings in town, and here I'd agreed to take care of these darlings for half price. They actually resided, I learned over time, at three fancy addresses—the Hamptons, Palm Springs, and Manhattan, in this sprawling apartment featured in the *New York Times* "Style" section. Since that day I found my kindness had been abused, I've had a sliding scale and won't give anyone rates until I've seen how nice their furniture is.

Some people are just naturally greedy and never have enough. Years down the road, still getting his undeserved discount and with no increases, my client with the cairns, groomed to look strikingly angular and blend with his art deco interior, called to ask if we "could work on the price." I reminded him he was already getting two-dogs-for-one. He backed off, as hagglers often do when you call them on their cheapness, their wish for the world to think they're rich trumping their taste for a deal. But for months after this latest attempt at a discount, he seemed unable to resist finding ways to squeeze more from each dollar he gave me. His self-esteem demanded it. Instructions for the boys' care grew more elaborate and exacting, with strict new guidelines set for measuring their food and supplements, and the precise times, down to the minute, for meals and walks while they were staying with me. He even started weighing the dogs, before and after their stays, then phoning to say they were "a little over" or "a little under" after I'd returned them.

One morning my client who ran a tight ship called from Paris to check on his waxing and waning cairns. He and his boyfriend were staying in a five-star hotel on the very elegant Place Vendôme, he said, and they'd just had the most amazing "French-Asian fusion" dinner at a fabulous four-star eatery on the rue Saint-Honoré. Before I hung up, I asked if maybe, when I brought the boys home in a few days, he wanted me to pass by the Chinese laundry on Sixth Avenue and have them weighed. To save him the trouble. His rate the next time, I added, would be double, the same as my other clients paid without all the added fuss. After all, I explained, this was only fair to everyone else.

He never "used" me again.

The cheap bastard with the cairns was a decorator and worked for a living, well, sort of. Rich kids with trust funds, just out of school but living large and in no hurry to get jobs, also need watching. Not to say their parents aren't good for the wages they owe me—they'll pay any amount I ask, when they pay—just that they have no idea what money's worth, what it's like to be without it, or the things normal people must do to eat. Like spoiled me in a previous life, they have everything comped for them, and constant reminders are needed to milk these pampered pets of my overdue utilities payments.

Privileged pups like these have been landing here in droves in recent years, in greater numbers than perhaps ever in the city's history, jacking up rents for all of us, exiling my working friends to Brooklyn, Queens, Staten Island, New Jersey, and the great desert beyond. After thirty-six years in this town, thanks to the security of a rent-regulated apartment, I now find myself surrounded by people richer than I'll ever be, the very ones I left my posh suburb to escape. They're quickly turning the whole city into a grand and bland Upper East Side, a neighborhood I've always hated. New arrivals are seldom interesting to get to know, but in my interest getting to know if they have dogs I can walk for sky-high rates.

Only the idle rich can afford to be truly nonchalant about money, and many of my new neighbors, though handsomely overpaid for their corporate jobs, still care about prices. They can be heard discussing stocks and mortgages in the local dog run, rather than having those heated debates over art and politics that used to fill the Village air. They talk about what preschools their kids just got accepted into, or how hard it is to find good help these days. By upscaling the city, these opulent executives and unemployed trust fundies have closed most businesses within reach of mere mortals in my neighborhood. They've replaced coffee shops and other humble eateries with designer posing salons where the point is not to eat but to look fabulous, and to show the world how they got to look that way: by not eating. Passing crowds observe as they sit at elegant sidewalk tables picking leisurely at miniscule meals, colorful, textured, artfully arranged with decorative sprigs of rosemary on enormous near-empty platters that make them, and their meals, look even skimpier. Everything on the menu seems to come with some sort of "reduction"—everything but the prices.

I've lived here too long to say New York isn't always changing. It always is, for better or worse, like it or not, though what has happened to the city in recent years has been extreme. I suspect a large part of the local economy, top-heavy with luxurious lifestylers, has long been artificial, a big empty bubble kept inflated by the idle consuming their nonessential goods and services, the rest of us scrambling to keep them coming. Outside money and labor piped in from all corners of the globe is what keeps the whole thing going, the fabulous restaurants, clothes, shops and shows, enticements for rich kids to stay and spend, and for the opulent executives, reasons to be overpaid.

Every imaginable desire is gorged at any time of day or night, including a lavish expenditure like me to walk a dog while little Miss Muffet sits on her ToDD HASE tuffet, eating her kale and weighing next to nothing. Where else but

New York could she lounge all day in a three-million-dollar apartment Daddy bought, until grabbing a small bite—just one—then hitting the clubs? She pulls up at dawn in an Uber car to take her French bulldog for a quick pee, crawls into bed until noon when I arrive and, hair messed and squinting like a vampire in the sunlight, she hands me a gold lamé leash at the door.

Working for the rich is one thing. Slaving for the rich and famous, I'd learn one day, is another. Once I was told by Madonna's handsomely-paid hairdresser, whose bouncy little lapdog of the white-and-fluffy genus I boarded, that some celebrities can be extremely neurotic and demanding, self-involved and snapping fingers to make everyone jump. This was just something you had to accept, he told me, or not bother working for celebrities.

I'll go a step further and say that supporting the indulgences of the rich and famous, or even just plain rich, you enter into an unspoken agreement. The rules are different in the stratosphere where you have the rare privilege of charging society prices. Little is it known down on earth, the ultimate reason for well-to-do clients having too much money for anyone's wellness is not just to spend, but to use an upper hand to assign blame for anything in their lives not coming out as planned.

Take one inbred hairdo of a dog—please—I walked for many years, also of the white-and-fluffy genus and called a Coton de Tulear. Packaged as "The Royal Dog of Madagascar," the consummate lapdog—with a coat so fragile it must be brushed and bathed very carefully or be tangled and sheared, as I learned trying to do one client a favor—this is the fake-historical type Barbara Streisand had cloned. The Coton in question, aptly named "Princess," had the less than regal habit of shitting where she slept, or rather, where the kids slept, among a wide range of other bad behaviors. After all the money they'd spent, the filthy-rich family who'd invested in the messy hairball assumed she was like any other temperamental, high-priced gadget: If she didn't work right, then it had to be someone else's fault.

The ill-bred Coton's owners' only saving grace, in my eyes, was in never trying to return their dog, or to throw her out, as many people do when they realize a lapdog is not a lap*top*. They never gave up poor little misbehaving Princess, but they did spread the blame for her naughtiness as far as their spending power could. Princess was given a celebrity dog trainer, the same who referred me to escort her out to pee and poo, if only Princess would. Two years later, having spent tens of thousands on at-home training lessons, and done nothing in the way of follow-up themselves, the owners kept expecting this confused hairdo of a hound to be magically domesticated. Surely, they said when their adult dog was still "making" in the house, and biting visitors and staff, it wasn't because they hadn't followed a single instruction the trainer left—they hadn't—after endless private sessions (which helped the trainer to buy a vacation home Upstate). No, this lack of social graces could only be blamed on the trainer for refusing to move in with the family for as many years as it took to house-break their precious little Princess.

This dog wasn't all bad, and when she was it wasn't her fault. After so much tutoring, Princess did know how to "sit" on command, and she had mastered a few amusing tricks like "roll over" and "play dead," so long as a treat was part of the bargain. The fruits of her long and costly education stopped there. Here was a dog with almost every problem money could be thrown at, and for some strange reason, the poor thing was still a royal mess. Her owners, in their own minds, had done everything right. They'd gone to one of society's most "repu-table" breeders, and not only was their superior purchase dis-obedient, but a family history of inbreeding meant she was always sick. Her list of ailments must have been the society veterinarian's fault, they reasoned, for not finding the right combination of meds when they arrived at his Park Avenue office each week with some new complaint (and more money to add to his kids' college funds).

The children who got Princess as a Christmas gift weren't much better behaved than their ill-bred dog, but at least they'd been potty-trained by the live-in nanny. These kids were always on the go with their thousand-dollar leath-er Armani backpacks and four-hundred-dollar New Balance sneakers. They went to the finest private schools, and at home they were far too busy to walk their own dog. An endless procession of French and math tutors, the piano teacher, the dance and yoga instructors, the hairdresser, manicurist, pedicurist—a long line of contracted servants left little time for tending to their dog's business.

That was where I came in, through the same back door as the rest of the servants. In time, the mistress of this out-of-control household decided to fire the dog's society trainer for not doing her job. The blame for Princess not doing hers was reassigned, the full weight of it, to me, her society walker.

Now, to earn the big bucks, I ate more than my fair share of shit for Princess still not being house-trained by the ripe old age of five. This pathetic creature hadn't a clue. Each day, after a pointless hour-long promenade as her official chaperone, I returned the pooch with nothing positive to report, taking my money but getting looks. Princess had things ass-backwards and was doing the opposite of what we wanted. Handing her leash to the nanny or cook at the servants' entrance, I knew very well where she would run the moment they let her. Rather than go outside like a normal dog, she'd been saving her business, numbers one and two, for the children's rooms where she squatted squarely on their carpets and "made," as her owners continued to say euphemistically despite the mounting unpleasantness. Several carpets later, and with a full walk-in closet housing an enormous collection of designer leashes (every year replaced, valued for tax purposes at a hundred dollars or more each, and donated to animal charities that would have preferred kibble and blankets), my clients still weren't wondering what they were doing wrong, but what *I* wasn't doing right.

My reputation was at stake. Rich people know each other and rumors spread. Short of trying to squeeze Princess like a lemon, or to coax a golden turd from her backside, I was at a loss. The trainer's lesson plans long since shredded and recycled, the proprietors of Princess decided on another strategy. They would pay me to walk their dog indefinitely, at least until something came out where we wanted and I could report my mission was accomplished. Money was no object to these people, but it was for me, and for many moons I paid my rent, and then some, by dragging Princess around for six, eight, ten hours each day. She stared blankly at my other dogs as they gladly evacuated around trees and off curbs. She was utterly baffled, and even seemed a bit snobbish about "making" in public. Was this some party to which she wasn't invited, some joke she wasn't let in on? The sun set and I returned the uncooperative canine, tail between my legs but hand open, to her highly-appointed house wishing I had better news. To the end of her days, long after the children had left their reeking rooms to do activism at Ivy League schools, this dog ran directly upstairs and "made" as tradition demanded. The Princess without the pee—at least not where we wanted.

Spending so much of one's life worrying about the bodily functions of other people's pets, some may say, is hardly a pursuit for an educated person. No matter how vital and valued we are as caretakers to the centers of their lives, some people still think of dog walkers as lowly sanitation workers. Anyone with the slightest bit of imagination should know that what I lower myself to do for dear friends is about much more than picking up poop or encouraging pees. Serious business this is, nonetheless, and when whizzing works right, it's a wonder to behold.

Going out for walkies is no more fun and games for my crew than it is for me. Not simply for relief, evacuating can be a vital source of self-expression to dogs, a powerful tool for communicating with their kind. My pups may meander but they're on a mission. What they express in ways we find revolting remains a mystery, though we're fairly certain that with each new post in liquid or solid they share sophisticated data on social standing, gender, breeding status and more, and simply by lifting a leg for high marks or squatting strategically to dump on someone else's personal profile. Whether it's surfing the sidewalk with a trickle of tweets to post on lampposts and trees, making the rounds to check for peemails, territorial pissing in a moment of inspiration—or excreting weightier statements—shameless self-promotion and one-upmanship are driving forces in this town, whether you're human or canine. For dogs, going "to the bathroom" is not a private matter to be hidden or ashamed of, but a public act as blatant as those gigantic messages scrolling across surfaces in Times Square. The higher the mark, the bigger the splash. Wolves, my dogs' ancestors, it has been said in ink and pixels, would spray from treetops if they could, not unlike our corporate top dogs with their stilted skyscraping.

In a way, I'm the publicist for my dogs' official releases. I may not be able to make sense of their scents, but respect this constant need to get the word out, if only to say: "I'm still here, alive and kicking. Take note, all ye who pass and piss." If I were canine, I'd be concerned if someone came along and messed with my messages, as in comment sections to my published articles where any idiot has a voice. And yet I'd be offended if no one bothered marking me up. So high is my esteem for a *provocateur* pup trying to elicit some reply, it trumps petty concerns like sparing decorative shrubbery and brownstone facades, lost causes some neighbors have made their life purposes to uphold against all odds. Many times have I been chased, dogs trailing behind, by irate gardeners whose pathetic ivy patches we've just watered, or doormen running, fists clenched and fuming over front entries just hosed down, only to be hosed again.

As in any serious literary endeavor, getting messages across city surfaces can't be isolated from questions of style. Should one squat or lift a leg? And if the latter, then how high is high enough? Contrary to popular belief, I've known males to pee daintily on all fours, releasing rivers of gold that make their way to the gutter. Wasted efforts. Many females, on the other hand, are leg-lifters in league with the top guns. Regardless of gender, some dogs piss volumes but infrequently, others nonstop in small vignettes. Some are straight shooters while others beat around bushes. Males are generally the biggest pains in the ass to walk, especially if unneutered. Every step of the way they stop to investigate, holding back my pack with their sniffing and pausing, assessing what's been said and how to elaborate. It's baffling how these canine camels carry these endless reservoirs around to graffiti the city. "Did all that come outta *you*?" I sometimes ask. I look at my watch while the males stop a fifteenth time, then circle to approach from a new angle and make another point. They lift a leg to fire blanks for effect when other males are passing. They backtrack the next day to spots they've marked to dot their *i*'s and cross their *t*'s.

Along with styles of canvassing, there's also the vital question of venue. Where and what should one mark? Urban centers are concentrated with urine and feces brought to the public square in gallons and tons each day. From a dog's over-stimulated perspective, New York is awash with information, layer upon layer of messages begging to be deciphered then covered with fresh dispatches. OCD posting can make dogs as neurotic as bipeds over-texting on their handheld devices, those chatty New York know-it-alls always saying something but seldom very much.

I pity pooches returning from stays in the wide-open country where untouched surfaces are aplenty and it's easier to stand out from the crowd. Marking fields and forests is less frenzied with more time for reflection and more blank slates to go around. Back in town, dogs are under the gun again to get the news out, overwhelmed by this saturation that passes for knowledge, and rising above the stench to make themselves heard must sometimes seem futile. Arriving from their cottages Upstate, or beachfront property on Long Island, some of my dogs must be watched closely at corners or will lift legs on pedestrians waiting for lights to change! Replies have not been pretty. I know a pug with a place in the Hamptons who'll douse anything standing, but who sniffs at fire hydrants which he considers clichés.

I've followed the blogs of my dogs since they were pups whizzing on Wee-Wee Pads or the nearest rug. I've shared proud moments as they've unlocked the powers asleep in their loins, learning to save their business for outdoors and using every drop wisely. A cute little guy I took on at three months, a breed becoming fashionable, a border terrier named Logan— the pup I wouldn't let that mobster chick pet and got my life threatened over—was squatting like a girly dog when he first joined our pack. Housebroken, more or less, Logan seemed painfully aware of some higher purpose to peeing still not revealed to him. He sniffed with fascination at tree trunks and corner curbs and I smiled at his fledgling attempts. Sensing something pertinent needed saying but unsure quite what or how, he crouched *near* signposts and fences but not exactly *on* them, comical misfires that endeared him to me all the more. As time passed, Logan edged closer to his targets, still not lifting a leg but discharging in dirt with a frustrated look on his scruffy black face. Eager the next day to return to the spot for another shot, he sniffed to size up the situation, then with one hind leg trembling under his weight and the other half-cocked—just high enough to wet all over himself—he finished up and took the Walk of Shame to rejoin our pack.

This went on for months. Then came the day my terrier friend, an adolescent now, finally learned to walk with the big dogs. The very morning Logan was scheduled to lose his manhood to a local veterinarian, he looked upon a tree across the street with the stiffened resolve of a young man who at long last summons the courage to ask a young lady to dance. Chaperoned safely by me through traffic and addressing his ambition squarely, he made his final approach.

No one ever taught this lad how to make his mark in the world. This was something he'd seen the other dogs do but had to learn himself. After months of misfires and without the slightest hesitation, suddenly as though a matter of routine handled summarily a thousand times before, Logan confronted that tree trunk to take charge of his surroundings. He flung his right hind leg mechanically into a salute, the left planted firmly on the ground and bearing his weight confidently. He held it there, at a full ninety degrees, and added those two cents he'd been saving for so long.

"Good dog!" I cheered, passersby wondering why, the other dogs wagging their tails out of habit when hearing these words. My small pal had finally hit pay dirt, and he was right on the money. "Yes! Hooray for *you*!" I told my triumphant terrier whose own tail was wagging wildly. Mission accomplished, knowing something quite right had just been done, Logan wasted no time strutting the sidewalk in search of the next spot to mark. A new dignity to his gait, a rite of pissage behind him, he embarked upon a journey that would last a lifetime.

CHAPTER NINE

When you've been outdoors pounding the pavement for fifteen hours or more each day, always on the move, seven days a week for more months than you can remember, you begin to lose perspective. Yesterday and today merge with tomorrow, your last step slides into the next, and your mind begins to wander.

There's even a condition that sets in, or one that I've discovered and self-diagnosed. I call it "dog walker's vertigo." This is when I've been pushing forward nonstop for hours, eyes open for dangers to my wards, feet and legs aching, wrists tied tightly with any number of leashes in leather or cloth, dogs doing their best to huddle as a pack on the trail but whose combined mass leaves me feeling unhitched. Dizzy and trying to focus on the curb after a series of separate outings, I sometimes start confusing the dogs' names, or worse, forget which ones I'm walking, and need to look down at their sweet faces watching trustfully for their next move.

Pausing to catch my breath and re-coordinate our bearings is just what the doctor ordered. Perhaps I'll duck into an air-conditioned bodega, if they're not opposed to dogs, watching closely for the store cat whose failure to fear has resulted in pandemonium on a few occasions. A cold soda for me, and a communal lap from a large water bowl placed out front by the kind shopkeeper, and we're recharged and back on track. Or maybe I'll need more than refreshment, like sitting on the stairs to a brownstone townhouse, panting in the shade in concert with my friends until the owner chases us away.

The day in question was in winter, though unseasonably warm. Dog walker's vertigo, or DWV, was setting in as I glided glassy-eyed down West Fourth Street with my gang of four (or was it five?) to take time out for everyone's safety. My mission an empty stoop sighted a few doors down, in my periphery I noticed a row of snowdrifts, or rather snow piles from a recent shoveling, melting away in the sun on this oddly torrid December day. Sweat dripping from my brow and blurring my vision, I looked down to guide my followers up the stairs we'd occupy for a few minutes—and remembered I was wearing cargo shorts and a T-shirt.

The snow lining the street hadn't even registered. The film crew and lights reminded me it wasn't winter at all, but a dog day afternoon of August—or was it Christmas in July? West Fourth Street, in my thirty years of living on it, had been the backdrop to dozens of movies, television shows, fashion shoots, advertisements, probably hundreds but I stopped counting. Al Pacino once camped in my doorway for a couple days. Then there was the night I went to get my bike, leashed out front to a signpost, and make my next dog-walking gig.

Crouching with my keys, I opened the padlock and grabbed the chain, then rose to find myself standing face-to-face with John Turturro who'd stuck his head through the trailer door at that precise moment. He looked as startled as I must have.

Another time, early one winter morning—real winter, not staged—my pups and I were perambulating past an old haunt on Fourth called "Almost Joe's," which is no longer but where something big was happening. The place aglow with harsh lights and packed with people hours before it normally opened, I peeked in the window just as Gene Wilder looked out and his gaze locked with mine. The comic's breath was steaming the other side of the glass, though not enough to hide his face, or the big ski sweater he wore and the coffee mug he held. I must have flinched in groupie astonishment because Wilder did the same, parodying my wide-eyed, jaw-dropped look of surprise like a mime artist.

Just when I thought I couldn't get more starstruck, Mike Myers, living somewhere nearby, started laughing each time I rode by on my bike with several dogs, including my own dear Samantha, all of them trained to run alongside in perfect "heel" positions. My amazing circus act, minus the tutu, the greatest show on earth (at least in downtown Manhattan), is still imitated, but I'm the one who did it first. You can ask Mike Myers.

Of course there's always a danger in living your life on a stage set. If not careful, you'll get an inflated sense of your own importance and otherwise ordinary things can be blown out of proportion. To avoid getting his ego overstuffed or super-sized, actor Jeff Daniels once said in an interview, when not working he preferred to live in Chelsea (not Manhattan, but a farm town in Michigan where my grandmother used to take me in her pickup truck to shop at the five-and-dime). Stars who move to places like New York or L.A., Daniels explained, get all snooty and self-absorbed, and before they know it are [he makes a gesture as though patting his hair].

Guilty as charged, though I was no star when I got here. From the time I moved to the Village, I was consciously aware of the possibilities for growing larger than life and the opportunities I wanted to embrace. So many nobodies had become legends simply by living on the stage I crossed daily. That guy from the Village People started dressing as an Indian long before the band was formed. Rollerena the drag queen spent years skating up and down Christopher Street before he/she was immortalized at Studio 54. And who could forget the crazy lady who played her bugle every morning in front of the coffee shop on Sheridan Square where I had breakfast (now, like everything else, a Starbucks)? She never became famous, but old-time Villagers remember her well.

Likewise for Andy Warhol's whole cast of characters, sideshow oddities that would have been left out of history had they not been self-promoting in the right place at the right time. Early on, I surveyed that familiar landscape with scenes from so many movies I'd seen, awestruck before its power and eager to unlock its secrets. All the world's media shared those very same sidewalks with the locals, waiting with notepads, microphones, and cameras to record our every move and capture the birth of every trend. It was as plain as the nose on my face that if you were in the least bit eccentric and willing to put in the time, if you had the patience (and the rent-controlled apartment to stay on location), if you had the discipline to stick with it and stay in character, eventually you'd be known if not renowned. If a name was what you lived for—or perhaps immortality?—it was really just a matter of waiting.

This would explain why New York is so overcrowded with big egos, performance artists, and conceptual environments installed, and world-famous, if only in New York. The most unremarkable things, and everyday lives, are called art here, and without much effort. Mundane details, however small and insignificant, get puffed up like balloon characters the night before the Macy's parade. It's naïve to believe that half the crap that passes for "important" would even be noticed without being in the right context. I hardly think that dumping a truckload of dirt in my grandma's Michigan farm house would be world news. In New York, they call it the Earth Room and it has major funding.

During those long years of awaiting recognition and begging to be discovered, I unwittingly pulled off an earthy performance piece of my own, one that my neighbors, a captive audience, couldn't miss if they wanted.

Every Christmas I like to buy my clients' dogs gifts, and a new shop on Greenwich Avenue was selling cute little bags of red and green bone-shaped biscuits tied with red and green ribbons. I could not have known, and my clients were not happy to find, the treats were a bit too rich for some tummies, and between Christmas and New Year's mass diarrhea ensued. Village curbs and corners were decorated, in that upsetting time, with festive swipes in green or red, or some blend thereof, long slicks of tinted liquid feces that could not be fully scooped no matter what the law demanded. Impromptu strokes by my own expert hand rivaled the rest, truly inspired, I must say, surpassing the boldest works of gesture and mark by master Japanese brush painters of centuries past, or New York's Abstract Expressionist School whose members used this neighborhood to act out their own legendary lives. An established poop performance artist of some importance now, living, breathing, dog-walking proof that even bodily functions can be art if things come out at the right time and in the right place, I'm thinking of applying for a federal grant.

Or maybe I'm taking all this context too seriously. Another helpful warning: If you're surrounded by celebrity and conscious that every inch of concrete you cover is ladened with something important that once happened there, or is about to, it's hard not to be full of yourself. Does this mean all

New Yorkers are vain opportunists, phony Holly Golightlies parading around name-dropping, thinking they're hot shit for doing not much, but for not doing it in the most famous city in the world? Tempted to take this cynical view, I know in my heart that some things are real in this place where everyone's on cue for a line and ready for their next close-up.

One brisk November afternoon while out with my sweet Samantha, a lovely shepherd mix puppy of six months from the ASPCA, I learned that if New Yorkers can be pretentious, outside voyeurs shouldn't be too harsh on us. Sometimes, despite all our props and accessories, and the condescending glares at hicks who've never heard of the Earth Room, we can be as genuine and earnest as any nobody living nowhere. We can even be endearing if given a chance.

Before our walk on that November day was done, I turned off Hudson Street and let Sam run off-leash for an hour with some other dogs on an enormous baseball field made of red sand, a favorite place for them to meet. Behind us, on the other side of a concrete wall, was the outdoor public pool I used in warmer months. This was the setting for the scene in *Raging Bull* where Jake LaMotta, played by Robert De Niro, meets the love of his life—a film I saw for the first time one summer day at a theater a block away, only minutes after swimming in that very same pool and with my hair still wet.

Done with our playdate, Sam and I exited the ball field through an iron gate, walked by a famous bocce court, then sauntered along a shady stretch of Leroy Street where Audrey Hepburn's character, a blind woman being terrorized by a ring of heroin dealers, was supposed to have lived in a film called *Wait Until Dark*.

We looped around a few blocks and made our way up Sixth Avenue where a famous joyride scene in *Mean Streets* was shot. Crossing Waverly where Robert Redford and Jane Fonda resided in *Barefoot in the Park*, we edged along the north side of Washington Square, a spot painstakingly reconstructed in a studio to look as it might have in the nineteenth century for the film version of a Henry James novel with Olivia de Havilland, Montgomery Clift, and Ralph Richardson. We passed under the familiar arch that announces Fifth Avenue, but were stopped by a guy wearing a headset. A roar came down lower Fifth as hundreds of panicked pedestrians rushed screaming through the arch and stumbled into the park fountain. They dragged overflowing shopping bags and half-opened suitcases packed like they were trying to leave town in a hurry, perhaps to escape King Kong, or just to escape from New York. Huge, generator-powered fans sent papers, leaves and clothes whirling into the air, enhancing the sense of chaos for something called *The Day After Tomorrow*, the flyers posted on parking signs said.

Years later, when Sam and I were both starting to grey, we approached Washington's arch again, and I noticed patches of weeds and piles of rubble that hadn't been there the day before. The scene I'd recognize later on the big screen when I saw *I Am Legend*. Will Smith was running with his faithful shepherd mix, a dog like mine, to take refuge in the fortress he'd made of a historic home on that same north side of the square, not long after the world had ended.

My puppy and I cut diagonally across the park and headed back home along West Fourth. We passed the place where Jimi Hendrix once lived, then stopped at our building on the corner of Jones Street where a famous Bob Dylan album cover was shot. Down Jones, to the left, was the funky building Al Pacino's character occupied briefly in a film called *Cruising*, the row of trees out front mere saplings in the 1980 pan shot. Before getting out my keys, I paused in front of our building, my bike hitched to the spot that would earn it a cameo appearance in *New York, I Love You*.

A light snow was coming down. This was Sam's very first and I didn't want her to miss it. Intrigued by the white dust collecting on the sidewalk, she lowered her head and sniffed—then sneezed, and I fell in love with my puppy all over again.

Driven by a force that needs no explaining, I squatted to Sam's level and hugged her with all my might. About to rise again, I sensed a figure to my right standing, looking down. A man, I knew without raising my head, had witnessed the whole tender scene and squatted beside us. Drawn into the magic of an unrehearsed moment, he patted Sam on the head, enthralled as I was by my girl with her trusting regard and awkward ears. I saw the stranger's face from the corner of an eye, and without staring I knew this was Sam Shepard who'd also just fallen in love. We said nothing, just kept crouching over the pavement in silent awe of the creature of beauty and innocence seated between us who was unaware she swept snow from the sidewalk with her wagging tail.

CHAPTER TEN

About ten years into my sidewalk odyssey, I started to worry about the future. I'd come too far to turn back and find a normal job. What if I never made it as a writer, but stayed just a dog walker, and then for only as long as my body could take? I'd watched the old-time walkers, who like me had probably set out with other plans in life. These gnarly characters limped by, feet dragging, backs hunched and barely able to walk themselves much less the ten or twelve dogs tied to their arms. Hopes and dreams forgotten, they were always getting into fights with people on the sidewalk, screaming at the top of their lungs and not caring what anyone thought. Their faces looked older than they should have after decades of sun and wind and cold. Always on the move, I sometimes caught a glimpse of myself reflected in a shop window and could see I was headed in the same direction.

So for a time I tried to set my sights higher than the gutter and flirted with the idea of advancing from dog walker to dog trainer. It was physically demanding work, but less than what I was doing, and the pay would have been more. Another way dog walkers like to diversify and increase their income is by going to school for grooming. I liked the idea of extra cash, but respected dogs too much, even the silly froufrou breeds, to have a hand in subjecting once-noble creatures to the further indignities of perfume, powder, outlandish bouffants, and pink polka dot bows. I chose instead to apprentice with a well-known celebrity trainer who sadly turned out to be a bad match and turned me off to training—but that's another story.

I really did seem to have the gift you need to be a good dog trainer and sometimes regret my move to being a dog writer instead. I found I had a natural knack for communicating, kindly and gently but clearly and forcefully, what I wanted done and not done. The dogs watched me. They listened. They understood.

My favorite type of training work, I discovered early on, was the hardcore stuff. Trying to turn around dangerous dogs was much more interesting than housebreaking, and made sit, stay, and play dead look like a cakewalk. I cut my canine teeth on several aggression cases, all ranging in severity. These troubled souls' owners had the money, time, and love to try and help their dogs get better, to teach them how to live in a human world and play by our rules, instead of just putting them down, as many do. The thought of saving animals whose very lives depended on changing their acts was only part of the allure for me. I soon acquired a taste for the rush of adrenaline—first felt when meeting my friend Gracie, the reluctant Rottweiler—that came with handling the biggest, strongest, least predictable dogs. They knew as well as I that we were both putting on an act, me pretending to believe I made them respect me, them pretending to be under my spell. They could have, without a moment's notice, instead of turning themselves around, turned on me and done some serious damage. Meager canvas straps around their snouts, even sturdy metal muzzles, were uncomfortable but not insurmountable. The symbolic piece of string I dangled—the leash—was hardly holding them back. On a whim, a willful pupil could get bored with being plied with liver treats as rewards, and promises for more if they kept complying. Our little game of master and slave could end if they decided to keep things real.

During my brief time training aggressive dogs, I had the honor of getting into the head of one giant fellow, a German shepherd/Newfoundland cross named Leroy who lived in nearby Soho. A genuine predator, this guy liked to single out small children on the sidewalk, then lunge at them, teeth bared and no holds barred. Any tragedy would have been for all involved, because if Leroy hurt someone he'd be taken away and destroyed. He was especially fond of the elderly. A limp added spice to the hunt.

My assignment was to keep this testy carnivore on a fifteen-foot lead I stretched, like a spider's web, across a busy square at Prince Street and Sixth Avenue, awaiting volunteers to step up, unknowingly, and help save this dog's life with some reconditioning. While pretend prey passed unaware, I kept my large, shaggy friend focused on my voice, higher and softer than normal to calm him, and on my bulging pocket of freeze-dried liver treats he got only by sitting quiet and still while the juicier morsels got away. The slightest growl from deep within his barrel of a chest—I could feel the vibration at the other end of my pathetic piece of string—and he got no prize but had to wait for the next chance to show me what a good boy he could be when he wanted. I had to keep a constant lookout for new ways to up the ante, to mix it up so Leroy learned to resist his darker impulses in many situations, in crowded public places of all kinds.

The whole city became our guinea pig with the powerful bargaining tool of liver treats I carried, and a clicker device to mark each moment. I guided Leroy toward children on sidewalks then steered him away, popping payoff in his mouth when he ignored them and clicking at the same time. As we waited on corners for someone, anyone, to pass, one freeze-dried-over-fresh trade-off was an old nun with a walker and orthopedic shoes returning to a nearby convent. She was so slow and helpless, almost comically unaware she was being stalked, and staying on her tail nearly emptied my pocket. Scary and irresponsible as my work must seem to the squeamish, they can rest assured that no animals, human or non-human, were ever harmed in the making of this very good boy.

People can be naïve about dogs, often deliberately. The sight of a cute face on a cuddly critter reduces the most sober adult into a babbling idiot eager to overlook any facts not feel-good, to deny even personal experience with dogs, because they can't give up that dopamine-induced trip back to their own innocent childhood days of puppy love. While so many insist on treating dogs as plush stuffed animals with button eyes, science reveals more and more about the true complexity of these feeling, thinking beings who, yes, form strategies and make choices, who possess what has been called a faculty for fairness and morality, but who also act by their own doggy natures. Rather than be demystified by new knowledge, diehard baby-talkers do our friends a real disservice by seeing them as hapless idiots bouncing through life blamelessly, goofy court jesters put here to entertain, props to reaffirm their belief in pure, unspoiled goodness, on the one hand, and the evils of human society on the other. It doesn't matter what horrible things some dogs do, and blind faith explains why the fact that breeds fluffier than pit bulls can be quite difficult is a hard pill for some to swallow. Like so many "others" cast into the victim class in recent years, dogs simply cannot err in the eyes of their apologists, not even when they hurt people, and other dogs, over and over again.

I've lost new clients by refusing, in no-pussy-footing terms, to take their Shiba Inus, adorable-looking Pokémon characters, into the local dog run where, not without good reasons, every single one of these antisocial animals has been permanently banned. The owners call me "racist" for "stereotyping an entire breed," but I challenge anyone to find a Shiba who has lasted longer than a few minutes in a dog run before tearing into another dog whose only crime was wanting to get acquainted.

I also tell inquiring customers I can no longer board cocker spaniels, a breed with big, wide cartoon eyes and long eyelashes like the saccharine animated character in Disney's *Lady and the Tramp*. Ambassadors of this irresistibly *cuuuuuute* breed, also known for something called "cocker rage syndrome," have made me turn their owners around on the Long Island Expressway to come collect their precious darlings pronto. "I just don't understand it," they say. "He's *never* done that before," they claim after droopy-ears has just punctured the tongue of a puppy bleeding profusely and savaged another dog. That's what they all say, until you learn their babes in the woods have long histories of violence they lied about before leaving on vacation.

Believe it or not—and you probably won't if you're a dog lover in denial—golden retrievers are now considered a potentially aggressive breed to be closely watched. I spent three months nursing a small Tibetan terrier, sent directly to me from surgery at a local animal hospital, because a golden, from the same home, had nearly ripped his leg off over a chewy treat. Humans also need to steer clear of this golden on the street, and taking her into a dog run is out of the question.

Another golden who "would never hurt a fly" was, within fifteen minutes after arriving in my home, trying to kill any dog for wandering too close to *his* water bowl in the kitchen. Another phone call and a turnaround on the Long Island Expressway.

I'm sure her mom and dad could have at least tried resisting the Jack Russell terrier puppy who sat in a pet shop window on Sixth Avenue looking like a harmless wind-up toy. The couple *bought* Maddie—contrary to popular opinion, pet shop windows don't typically offer "rescues" or "adoptions"— as many *buy* puppies, partly on impulse during a Saturday afternoon stroll, but also as part of a plan to use the puppy to practice at being parents together. I respected them for not throwing out their surrogate baby with the bathwater when the real deals arrived, as many couples also do. Mom had taken fertility pills, along with half the middle-aged women in my neighborhood overcrowding the sidewalks with their two-, three-, and four-headed baby carriages, pushing me and my crew off the curb, and turning local restaurants into Romper Rooms overrun with crayons, coloring books, and obnoxious screaming toddlers.

My client had twins, and Maddie the Jack Russell was displeased at first. She would learn, with time, to love and guard the children, but for now they were shrieking prey begging—WARNING: DISTURBING IMAGE—to be eaten, as infants have sometimes been by dogs. This certainly wasn't the picture of the faithful canine companion teaching their youngsters about life this couple had in mind. Watching Maddie around these colicky kids was alarming, to say the least. Anyone who has seen a crazed terrier's eyes go glassy— "fire in the eyes," the old-time hunting men call it when terriers switch to kill mode—knows what I mean. The infants' constant howling set off Mad like Pavlov's dog. She salivated and barked nonstop, emitting the most fiendish, chilling, agonized moan from her misleadingly tiny and adorable self. She sprang high, as Jacks do, as though on springs, trying to get into the bassinet. Her terrified and exhausted parents called the celebrity trainer, whose specialty was aggression, and me, her apprentice.

The lesson plan for Maddie was to come live with me for two months, during which time we became lifelong friends. (I know, wanting to eat children and all, but nobody's perfect.) My instructions were to engage her in intensive daily exercises to desensitize her to the babies' wailing. Mad moved in and brought with her a tape of the twins when they were really pissed off. I was told to play the recording, at increasing volume, while running her through rapid-fire commands. Mad kept working with me, but never did lose those glassy eyes while the background music was on. She strained, in great pain, it seemed, to act nonchalant and control her feelings. I doubt she was ever fooled by the rubber cartoon prop we used, that decoy baby wrapped in the twins' clothes and smelling of them, lying on a nearby table while Mad jumped through hoops for those liver treats.

It was no easy task for me to find a dummy kid in Manhattan, still a very adult place at the time. New York was only just beginning to be overrun by annoying brats, indulgent parents, daycare centers, upscale kiddie clothing stores, child barbershops, family values, and no more naughty words on the sidewalk. The Toys "R" Us store on Union Square back then was mainly for single people needing last-minute birthday or Christmas gifts for the offspring of friends and relations living anywhere *but* in the city. When career-minded yuppies who'd arrived with me back in the eighties started passing their primes and nearing the limits of their breeding years, they panicked and cheated with the new fertility drugs. But rather than move back to the suburbs to raise their families, the natural thing to do, they tried to make the city more like the suburbs. More and more, New York, that very adult place when I'd arrived and fun for that very reason, became juvenile. Playgrounds competed with dog runs for space in public parks. A new daycare center in the Village managed to block one much-needed dog run—enclosed, gated, and no threat to anyone—from being built a couple blocks away. Toys "R" Us became Babies "R" Us, a telling sign of new market demographics and these gaga times in which we now must live.

Before the invasion of family values, the old Toys "R" Us on Union Square didn't have a whole lot of decoy babies in stock, at least not the day before Maddie moved in and I needed one for her daily workouts. They only had black babies left, and I had no choice but to buy one.

My neighbors already knew I was weird. I got looks in the hall when they started hearing newborn infants crying in my apartment—"I thought you were single?" "I thought you were *gay*?"—and a dog moaning feverishly the whole time like a hound from hell. If they knew I was keeping a black baby doll in my icebox—the only place Mad wouldn't smell it and keep me up all night whining over it, the trainer told me— they probably would have called the cops.

More awkward for me than the looks of nosey neighbors, those months following Maddie's return to the bosom of her family cast new suspicions on my character. The twins had stopped their colicky crying by then, and to be scientific, I'd have to say there's no way to be sure the elaborate training I gave this dog had anything to do with her success back home. Maddie's parents were relieved to learn she no longer wanted to eat their twins, and overjoyed to know she actually adored her new brother and sister. Maddie dropped bouncy balls into the playpen to invite her siblings to play. She sat under their high chairs to eat whatever they'd throw. She stayed by their sides wherever they went, never taking her eyes off them (but in a good way). Making sure these kids were always safe became Maddies's new mission in life. The perfect pet completed the picture of a happy family—and my neighbors wondered what I'd done with those babies.

CHAPTER ELEVEN

Andy Warhol, or so I've heard, once said that in New York City we have no stars in the sky—because, he supposedly said, they're all on the sidewalk.

Though this does sound like something Warhol could have said, any seasoned dog walker, who spends more time on the pavement than just about anyone except homeless people, knows this isn't entirely true. Heavenly bodies are, indeed, seldom visible at night—they're eclipsed by reflections of the city's own lights into the atmosphere—but star sightings of the earthly kind are even rarer life events. If this weren't true, we'd probably yawn as they passed, which we do not. We wouldn't become giddy schoolgirls at the approach of Richard Gere or Liza Minnelli, which we do. We want the rest of the world to believe we've seen it all but we haven't, at least not yet. This is what keeps us here, paying outrageous rents for tiny one-room apartments and putting up with all the indignities: the outside chance of being brushed, once or twice in a lifetime, with stardust.

What were my chances of coming face-to-face with a supernova, my own boyhood idol, a bust from my personal pantheon—and being hired to walk his dog?

If they could see me now, I thought, that little gang of mine, rushing over on my bike to Lou Reed's apartment for an interview with his rat terrier.

A lot of people call them "fox terriers," but that's another brand. Many terrier owners can't bear the thought that their pets' ancestors were bred to kill lowly rodents, instead of hunting a prize with more upper-class resonance like, say, a fox or a stag. Ratting terriers were never even intended to be kept as house pets, and before they made it into front parlors of the rich and showy, they had no status appeal, except for exploits in the ratting rings. At first I was pleasantly surprised when the call came from Reed's assistant asking me if I might be able to walk and occasionally board his "rat terrier," with no attempt to invent some fake family tree. Maybe, I thought, the rock star, the role model of my youth, was a regular guy I could sit and chat with, not a god after all—but wouldn't that be a letdown?

I was exhilarated but terrified at the thought of meeting the inspiration for a song called "Queen Bitch" by David Bowie, who also seemed a bit afraid of Lou Reed. My stomach hadn't been right since I got the call, and before starting out on the bike for the interview, I put a few antacid tablets in my coat pocket in case of cramps. Reed may have been a god, but my nervousness was only human. How many mere mortals are given the chance to test an ideal, to hold an otherworldly standard up to the dreary, mundane light of an ordinary workday, at the risk of having it shattered forever? Here was the persona whose portrait I'd painted after a photo in a fan rag back in the seventies. Here was the guy Lester Bangs blamed in *Rolling Stone* for turning an entire generation of young men like me into "junkie faggot freaks." I couldn't, in all honesty, blame my sexuality on a time when so many rock stars were claiming to be at least bi because it sold records, but my druggie days were inspired in no small part by the belief that, if only I could be a bad boy, then maybe I could be Lou Reed.

The man wrote love songs to heroin, for Christ's sake. Everyone knew Reed had cleaned up his act since walking on the wild side, as I'd cleaned up mine, knowledge that doesn't make the fond memory of those grand, carefree times any less potent. I'd always been too young to remember the Velvet Underground, Andy Warhol's official band in the sixties with Lou Reed as front man. But I was just old enough in the seventies to be a punk rocker. By that time, Reed had transformed himself into something darker than the sixties had known. He had all the self-destructive qualities, combined with indefinite gender, that we punks found so seductive. He was our inspiration. I chopped off my George Harrison hair for him. I wore black leather. When asking my dad for the keys to the car in our posh Michigan suburb, I could only take my hands out of my pockets for a subliminal flash because my nails were painted black, like Reed's at the time, and my father would not have approved. A few lines of cocaine later, I was safely ensconced inside a seedy nightclub in downtown Detroit, in one of the most dangerous parts of what was then murder capital of the world, a fitting backdrop of urban decay, anger and despair, the same bleakness behind punk rock. A girlfriend put the finishing touches on my face in the ladies' room mirror, white pancake with black lipstick and black eye-liner. We punks, some of us working class kids who worked in factories, others rich kids like me in college, with our safety pins, chains, and spiked platinum hair, were sometimes shot at by passing cars. A friend once found a body in a back alley.

We weren't exactly New York but wanted to be. So we brought it to us. The CBGB bands played my club. So did the important British ones. Patti Smith was living nearby and I saw her standing by the stage whenever her husband of MC5 fame played. Bowie arrived one night, wearing a fur coat and two Dobermans, causing panic in Detroit. Mitch Ryder, a local rock star almost as famous as Reed himself but in awe of New York like anyone else, had changed the lyrics to one of Reed's most celebrated songs. "Then one fine mornin' she puts on a New York station. You know she couldn't believe what she heard at all … You know her life was saved by rock 'n' roll" became: "Then one day she hit that Detroit station …" A bold comparison to New York that no other city dared draw.

Twenty years later, I was flying across Sheridan Square not looking very punk in a U of M sweatshirt, ski jacket and jeans, longish hair, with a three-day beard (say what you will about those obnoxious punk rockers, they were always clean-shaven). I breezed past one of the last old coffee shops in the West Village where I'd stopped many times. Typical of coffee shops at the time, faded headshots of celebrities on the walls, supposedly signed by them, hung just below the ceiling like a Greek frieze, encircling this dive and hinting it was graced daily with the presence of Alan Alda and the Village People, who may have dined there but a very long time ago. It's that same long leap New Yorkers still like to take when implying some proximity, other than geographic, between themselves and the stars. The coffee shop would one day become a Starbucks, but the locals would still be speaking of the Great Ones in the most intimate, matter-of-fact terms, discussing "*Bob* Altman's last picture" or "*Marty* Sheen's first major role," as though they knew them personally.

Me and Lou? Harsh reality hit as I peddled toward the Hudson and the cold wind off the river smacked my forehead. I think I was more afraid of Reed not liking me personally than crushing any boyhood dreams about a persona. Wondering what I would say to him, I had a sickening thought of John Farley interviewing Paul McCartney on *Saturday Night Live* like an awkward adolescent groupie fumbling for words.

I saw Wayne and Garth kneeling before Alice Cooper and shouting "We're not worthy! We're not worthy!"

"Down boy," I commanded myself aloud. "You're only walking his dog," assuming he'd condescend to letting me in through the servants' entrance. Downstairs, next to the apartment number, was the name of someone called "Beginski." I pressed the button and a woman's voice beckoned me in.

I stepped off the elevator into a hallway that looked disappointingly like most any other in town. There was no star quality to the mundane interior of this typical industrial building converted into lofts. The walls were a dreary yellow, the doors normal, and on them numbers as finite as life itself. A relief it would have been to find the woman's voice on the intercom was that of a servant and I wouldn't have to meet Lou Reed at all. This happens with a lot of celebrities, or just rich people. A fellow mere-mortal from the staff and I work out, in the kitchen, the petty mechanics of what I must do, so the head of the household can attend to higher purposes, rarely dealing with or even seeing his or her own dog.

Some big personalities find the time to take a personal interest in the lives of their pets, and in who's being let in. They grow more protective of a dog or a cat than they'd be of their children, if they had them. Reed, I'd been forewarned, had already fired six walkers in the prior three weeks—a bit excessive, perhaps as much a symptom of a neurotic personality as any genuine concern for an animal—or so said the celebrity dog trainer who sent me over as cannon fodder for an-other shot. What on earth had all those other hopefuls done to get fired? Maybe they couldn't figure out how to play the game you need to play when working for superstars. Your job is to show unconditional obedience to their every command, no matter how demanding, absurd or self-involved, coupled with silent respect, not groupie bewilderment. For Reed's dog trainer, the woman who recommended me and a star in her own right, playing this game had paid off over the years. She started as a dog walker like me, and now she had special status in this town, working with all the best and brightest canines whose pictures glossed the pages of *People* magazine, even so-cializing with her clients. I'd found her waiting on street cor-ners for limousines to whisk her off to the Hamptons where she'd be paper-training some starlet's lapdog over the week-end and earning a nice piece of change in first-class accom-modations. She was on TV, and in penthouses of the rich and famous, or just plain rich, with interiors the rest of us buy *Architectural Digest* to see. She was the first of two celebrity dog trainers to give me work, but once confessed to me over dinner she was nothing special, as trainers go. "I'm really not that good," she said. She referred the difficult cases to less flashy colleagues who knew more about serious problems like aggression. "I just teach Al Pacino's dog to sit," she said, "and everyone thinks it's magic."

I held my breath and pressed the doorbell.

The door opened and I held my head down, not humbly, but because a little six-month-old rat terrier was jumping on me frantically. Black, brown and white, a fireball of energy and about as cute as a skinny pup can be, she catapulted herself off my jeans, leaving her invisible mark for other dogs to smell and helping me to relax. So much unbound joy and unrehearsed enthusiasm were the opiate I needed to soften the hard edge of a prickly New York moment. I finally looked up at what seemed the impish smile of a boyish young girl. This wasn't Lou Reed, or his assistant, but Laurie Anderson, the performance artist.

"It looks like you've made a friend," she said warmly and sweetly, sounding like my old Aunt Ceil. Her smile, the kind that takes over an entire face, was making me feel even more at ease. She looked down at her puppy, still jumping on me, the girl she'd one day put in a movie. Her face was lined with age and her short, choppy hair no longer made her look punk, though the smile was thirteen. "Looks like you've made a new friend, Lolabelle."

Laurie, Lou, and Lolabelle. You can't make this stuff up.

"You must be Michael."

There's something incredibly gratifying about having an immortal proclaim your name. It's one of life's greatest rewards, as though all your efforts and ordeals have been leading to this one supreme moment of recognition. Not to say you can't experience it more than once in a lifetime, if you live in New York. I had the same feeling when Holly Hunter came up to me one morning in the Washington Square dog run with her one-eyed Belgian shepherd named Larry, and thanked me for the volunteer labor I was doing there. Now I'd been given Laurie Anderson's validation. What a charmed life I was leading.

Laurie extended a hand and I prepared to touch a living legend. I'd worked for New York celebrities before, and I knew about the secret handshake. The in-crowd is a most exclusive club with an agreed upon greeting you should know when entering their circle of trust. An odd, limp grasp, more like a brushing than a handshake, is expected, like some royal protocol. The palms barely touch before the hands slide away and end contact respectfully, a far cry from the hearty Midwestern grasp I was raised to give to those whose trust I hoped to win.

"Come in," she said softly, gesturing me into a world I never thought I'd see, not as a servant or anything else. The puppy was eager to follow us back inside. The door closed and a few feet into the loft space was a second entry—perhaps as soundproofing?—a pair of enormous doors rising high to the ceiling. They appeared to have been torn from some Tibetan temple but could have been part of a stage set for a Frankenstein movie. Massive wooden slabs, blackened and riddled with spikes and chains, they'd work in any dungeon scene. To the right, beyond the dramatic portal, was a staircase, the pride of any Transylvanian castle, that turned and tapered toward some unseen chamber high above us. What Promethean shenanigans were underway up there? What dark forces being unbound? Reed's look has often been compared to that of the monster, and if it's true that glam led to punk, then it was a short step from science fiction to horror.

"Lou's almost done with his massage," Laurie said, looking to the top of the staircase where unholy things were perhaps happening. "Have a seat and when he comes down it'll be my turn so the two of you can get acquainted."

This was more than I'd bargained for, not one, but two interviews with someone famous. I reached inside my coat and felt for the antacid tablets then sat on the sofa. Lolabelle was all over me again.

"It looks like you have a wild pup on your hands. Mine's just turned two and she still hasn't started slowing down."

Laurie smiled and offered me something to drink.

"So how long have you been taking care of dogs?

"About two years now."

"Rhea says you do boarding. I'm going on tour in a few weeks and we could really use someone to take Lo."

"I'd love to have her. I have a small group of dogs who come over regularly. They're all good dogs," I repeated my standard sales pitch, which doesn't become any less true the more times I repeat it. "No aggression problems. Everyone plays nicely. When they're not playing, they're asleep at my feet while I write."

"And you do this in your apartment?" she asked, trying to imagine, like most new clients, what a Romper Room for dogs must look like.

Before I could answer, Laurie looked up the staircase, sensing before I did that a figure was descending from the unseen chamber on high. I felt my blood pressure rise with each step down by a being that seemed to float like Nosferatu. Real flesh and blood rounded the corner and landed squarely on the parquet floor in socks. Hair messed and face flush, a man appeared to be in that semi-dream state that follows a laying on of hands. A distinct potbelly emerged in profile.

That face. I'd studied it as closely as any groupie could and knew every inch. Since I'd painted his portrait twenty-some years before, the lines had grown more sharp and severe, recording a life lived hard and fast. Those haunting shark eyes hadn't changed.

I gently took Lolabelle off my lap and rose to offer my hand.

"I'm pleased to meet you, Mr. Reed."

That same limp handshake, then our eyes locked and he said nothing. He seemed to be looking right through me with his cold, dead stare, not smiling, or even pretending to be friendly, just keeping my hand in his with the slightest pressure for a few seconds longer than was conventional in his social circle. He slowly eased his hand away and his skin slid against mine, as though he was scanning me for information. This was creepy.

"Michael says he can take Lolabelle for us while—"

It was going to take more than that to win the trust of this tough cookie. The face remained blank, offering no clues, enough to keep me off-balance.

"How long have you been doing this?" Reed asked the usual question, though in a more rehearsed way than I was used to hearing. Perhaps he was trying to sound businesslike which seemed out of character. He sat down opposite me.

"I was just telling Ms. Anderson, about two years. I have a small group of dogs who come over regularly …"

Still no smile or sign for me to relax and speak freely as I repeated my spiel. My eyes wandering to avoid his glare, I noticed a small white square on a shelf. It was a CD cover for the same album I had at home on vinyl, bought with lawn-cutting money in high school back in suburban Detroit, but without the iconic airbrushed photo of Reed in makeup playing guitar. The title was printed in black, generic type: "Transformer Master." *Transformer* was Reed's most monumental album in the seventies, the one that saved him from the typing job he'd taken at his father's Long Island accounting firm after the Velvet Underground split up, thrusting him back into the limelight and the company of gods again. Bowie produced it and Mick Ronson wrote the arrangements. A masterpiece for those of us who like this sort of thing, it was since repackaged, reissued, marked down, punched, cut up, resold millions of times, keeping alive the legend seated before me who turned his gaze upon the whirling dervish on my lap. That almost looked like the smile of a proud parent.

"Will there be any other dogs in your place with Lo?"

"I usually have a couple. I get a lot of last-minute calls so I can't be sure. I've known all my dogs since they were pups like Lolabelle and we're all family."

"Do they ever have fights?" he asked, concerned as any dog parent should be.

"That's seldom happened in all my years of boarding dogs. I don't take any dogs with aggression problems. New dogs are sometimes nervous for a little while, but they set their boundaries and learn to fit in."

"Do *you* have a dog?"

"Yes I do. My Samantha's a sweet, gentle thing who wouldn't hurt a flea. She just loves puppies and I'm sure she's going to love little Lolabelle."

"Hear that, Lo? You're going to make some new friends," Laurie interjected in that high-pitched tone used to speak to small children and pets. I could feel some of the tension lifting from the room.

"She did the most amazing thing to my neck," Reed said, holding a hand behind his head. I didn't want to imagine how tense this interview would have been without the massage.

"It was nice meeting you, Michael," said Laurie, rising to climb the stairway to ecstasy under the same skillful hands. I got up but Lolabelle was too busy digging for something under a sofa cushion to notice her mom was leaving. She yanked out what looked like the remains of a stuffed animal of some kind, unidentifiable in its chewed, eviscerated, dissected state. The stuffing hung out and it had no eyes.

"We never say 'No' to Lolabelle," Reed said from out of nowhere. The gloves were off now that Laurie had left the room. He stared at his puppy with the mangled something hanging from her mouth. "And you shouldn't either."

I nodded in agreement but wasn't sure I could keep the promise. A nutty fringe of dog trainers fashionable in the city had taken "positive reinforcement" to extremes in recent years, to the point that you were no longer supposed to correct your dog with negative words, not even if they were misbehaving. This came with the new touchy-feely approach to child rearing which would lead to so many problems in a generation of hypersensitive brats. Like so many unsound ideas that become fashionable in New York, this spread like gospel to the world, and for no better reason than that a few nutty New Yorkers gave it the authority of scripture. In recent years, it has even become politically incorrect to call dog training "training," though no replacement term has been offered by members of this new school of dog trainers—or whatever they're supposed to be called—who chuckle when I still say "training."

"What's your apartment like?" asked the man who'd turned an entire generation of young men like me into …

Again, this question that comes up when new clients try to imagine what the Romper Room for dogs must look like, if only for the pleasure of knowing that such a wonderful place might actually exist. Reed wanted convincing. He sat stone-cold silent while I went on about how my studio apartment was large with good light, high ceilings, and plenty of fresh air. "All the electrical outlets and cords have been puppy-proofed. I have metal guards on the windows because a lot of New York dogs have chased pigeons off fire escapes." I told him how I gave up on rugs years ago because they were favorite peeing spots.

A slight change came over his face, as though he was pondering a new dimension he never knew existed.

"I'd like to come and take a look."

Rare is it when a client wants to actually see my apartment. Normally, my word is enough, mine and that of the celebrity dog trainer who referred me, solid gold in just about any book. I'm not insulted when they still want to take a peep into my strange and wonderful world. Lou Reed's offer to grace my home with his presence, if only to make sure my digs were nice enough for his rat terrier, was too seductive to turn down. Nobody was going to believe this.

"How much do you charge?"

That sordid topic of coin.

"Fifty a night."

Most people don't flinch at that figure, considering all they're getting. Reed gave me a look that said he couldn't believe anyone in his right mind would pay so much to board a dog, even though my rate was lower than commercial kennels where dogs were kept in cages.

"But I can go lower if that's a problem."

I seldom lower myself to haggling over rates, but I really wanted this gig, and it had little to do with money, an advantage I was sure had worked for Mr. Reed since he became a superstar with adoring fans.

"And for walks?"

"Well, they're covered with the boarding. So are pickups and returns. But if you'd like me to come over and just walk her, it's fifteen a half hour, twenty-five an hour. For that rate I guarantee not to walk any other dogs with yours. I prefer cash if that's not a problem."

At this point, most clients I'm landing say cash is not a problem. Not this one. Other people understand this is a cash business, not that I have anything to hide. I have an accountant and have been audited, and all is above board. Cash is just easier than checks, and with dogs to walk all day, I seldom have time to go to the bank. Reed wants to pay by check, he explains, because for some strange reason he can't understand, the IRS audits him every year and he needs to account for everything.

The man who spent years advertising to the world he was a drug addict, who called heroin "my wife," couldn't understand why the government had taken a special interest in his affairs. It looked like I'd be taking checks, and there was still another hoop to jump through.

"Maybe we should do a trial run and see how this works out," he said. "Can you walk her tomorrow at noon?"

"Sure, noon is fine," I answered without hesitation, not thinking about the client of three years whose Labrador retriever would have to wait an extra hour for his walk, and then all the other dogs whose times would also be pushed back. I felt some uncontrollable urge to find out what all those other walkers had done to get fired. I knew the last one, just before me, got herself canned for stepping on Lolabelle's paw—easy to do with a young puppy all over the place, but still—sending her off squealing. Reed was apparently fuming. What could all the others have done that I should avoid doing? I was honored to be the next in line to get shot down. In fact, I wasn't worthy.

We both rose and headed through the gigantic portal, stopping at the tiny and inconspicuous front door that from the hallway made this place look like any other apartment. I crouched to say goodbye to Lolabelle, then stood to find myself face-to-face with the legend.

He was everything he was supposed to be. He was a rock star, as big as they get. Outside, he was all tough and gnarly like a lobster. Inside, well, who knew? He was a little off when it came to everyday things that normal people do. Maybe it was all those drugs he did. Reed was blasé like his music, unfazed by the darkest corners of the city, the poetry of the street, the freak show of the New York underground he helped create. He never sounded overly impressed, only deadpan. I held out my hand to conclude our tentative deal. This time, he grabbed it tightly as though to take my pulse, piercing my soul with those dead shark eyes.

"If a single hair on her head …"

I flinched, visibly, I'm sure, and he didn't need to finish the sentence. This was not someone you wanted to mess with. I pulled away without saying a word and headed down the hall.

"Say goodbye to Michael," I heard from behind in a falsetto voice, turning to see Reed with Lolabelle in his arms. A boy and his dog? There was something rehearsed about that last line. Too cutesy. He was trying to parrot something he imagined Laurie saying.

Some things you can only know after living in a place for a very long time. Before I came to New York, I didn't understand a lot of Woody Allen's jokes. Now I get them all. You also have to live in a particular neighborhood of New York to have a true sense of it. I've been in the Village for decades, and still get a thrill from being brushed, as I've been quite a few times, with Andy Warhol's stardust, including the hand-me-down kind tossed around downtown by the wind off the Hudson River. It's frightening to ponder what an influence this man had. Not only did Warhol manage to hold captive the entire international art world, he moved through this neighborhood like a messiah anointing the chosen few—the chosen *many* would be more accurate, because hordes of downtowners were blessed with Andy's nod of approval. Whatever he gazed upon became special. If you had a gallery, you had to try and get him there on opening night if you wanted the world to follow. Andy also sought out people himself, the supreme compliment. A woman I knew on Eleventh Street made large handbags in the shapes of dogs, cats and other animals, elaborately detailed with colorful stitching. She lucked out one day when Andy showed up at her apartment, bought a few, and left his imprimatur on anything she made from that point forward.

Andy is also said to have been partial to the Polaroid snapshots by a guy who, for the longest time, sold them from a little card table erected on the sidewalk off Bleecker Street. His story wasn't hard to believe. Andy's imprimatur was given freely, and if his nod wasn't guaranteed to make you rich or famous, it gave you cachet for years to come. A woman I know on Fourth Street used to make dresses for Andy's drag queens. The guy living downstairs from me, a dear old friend since passed away, was in his films. The list goes on and on. Until the last of Andy's discoveries dies in a rent-controlled apartment chock full-o-memorabilia, downtown Manhattan will keep some of the stardust Andy left drifting about.

At 11:45 the next morning I was still feeling shaken by the previous night's threat. This had never happened to me. Most people saw my face and trusted me instantly. I peddled back to Reed's address on my bike, wondering how many more hoops would be placed in my path when I arrived. After several attempts from the street on the buzzer marked "Beginski," Reed's voice finally came over the intercom and he let me in. Off the elevator and down the same hallway, I stopped at the magic number and heard someone strumming an acoustic guitar somewhere deep inside the apartment. Pressing an ear against the door, I made out a chord change, a progression, then an abrupt stop and return to the first chord. Reed was composing.

Afraid to break the mood with an obnoxious doorbell, I finally gathered the courage to press the button. After all, he'd already buzzed me up and shouldn't have needed another alert to my arrival. The strumming continued. A jingling sound—percussion accompaniment?—started in the distance, growing louder then stopping at the other side of the door. Lolabelle was sniffing at the threshold. More strumming and still no answer. I didn't want to be pushy, but other dogs were at home waiting to be walked and I needed to get on with this. Did I dare press my luck and press the doorbell a second time? I recalled the story of the English poet whose wife once turned away some important visitor. She explained her husband was "in eternity" just now and could not be disturbed. Laurie was apparently not home, and so far Lolabelle was the only one excited to greet me.

Ten minutes passed, I was losing patience, and Lola-belle's enthusiasm had grown beyond containment. She started to whine and scratch at the door. The strumming stopped. The jingling resumed, faded out, then returned in full force. Three locks were turned from the inside and Lolabelle popped her pointy snout through the narrow opening, already attached to a leash held from inside.

I was moved by the sight before me. Reed stood with his puppy's leash in one hand, rigidly, his arm raised higher than would be comfortable, as though he was trying very hard to do something that didn't come naturally. He seemed afraid the little dog might break like a China doll if he wasn't careful.

Reed handed me the leash, swiftly but carefully, as if we were making a drug deal on the street.

"How long will this be?"

"A half hour. Unless you want a longer walk—"

"No. That's fine."

I turned to leave, and in that same falsetto voice, completely out of character, he said: "Have a nice time with Michael, Lolabelle." This was quite a contrast from the voice I'd known and loved all those years, and the jaded, seen-it-all attitude that made the hit "Walk on the Wild Side" such a masterpiece of New Yorkness. Not once did he break the mood in that song, always holding back, never losing his cool by going over the top with emotion, not even when announcing the chorus of "colored girls" (in reality, three white women).

I heard the door close behind me. Lo and I started down the hall, but I felt a tug on the leash. She was squatting on the doormat! Urine was running down the hall! I knew it wasn't my fault—who knew when anyone had last walked her—but I was afraid to bother Reed again. The guitar strumming had resumed, and I didn't want to awaken the artist from eternity, but something in the here-and-now needed attention.

Reaching for the doorbell, I heard another chord progression. This was really starting to sound like a song. Gotta do this. I pressed the button and the strumming stopped abruptly. The three locks were turned again and I held my breath, but Reed didn't seem angry over being disturbed, just blank, emotionless like his songs.

"Lolabelle's had a little accident," I reported nervously.

Reed looked at me like I was speaking Sanskrit, a dead language never actually spoken. What I said hadn't registered at all. I pointed down at the doormat and the small river meandering down the hall.

"Oh, you mean she got *excited*."

"Yeah." My throat cracked like an adolescent's.

Reed disappeared, returning with a roll of paper towels. I offered to clean up the mess but he didn't mind doing it himself, stooping to soak the towels with yellow liquid before it could migrate further. This was something I never imagined seeing in my lifetime: a rock star cleaning up dog urine from the floor. Lolabelle and I headed down the hall again, onto the elevator and into the street. Maybe this excited girl still needed to make number two ...

On the sidewalk, Lo acted like any other dog. Being a puppy, she was especially curious about everything in her path. The world must have been so new to her. New York pavement was the Great Outdoors, the call of the wild, maybe the only nature she knew. All those foul, familiar urban odors were Baudelairean perfume to her nostrils, and she darted from scent to scent as though following the trail of some small prey—rats, perhaps? I kept up the best I could, not expecting a dog so young to walk in a perfect "heel" position. She was looking for that perfect spot to do her business.

Lo and I rounded the corner and I saw a friend coming toward us. I couldn't wait to let him guess whose dog this was. I made all the predictable jokes—this was a "rock and roll an-imal" and we were taking "a dog walk on the wild side"—until a look of disbelief came over him.

"You really lead a charmed life, Michael."

"Seems so."

Lo and I continued down Hudson Street in search of that just-so spot to poo, and I decided to take her to a street a few blocks away that all my dogs seemed to like. Lo final-ly stopped at what appeared to be that perfect place, a small patch of earth surrounding a sickly tree that wore a hand-written sign scrawled, in a moment of desperation by some member of a block association: "Curb Your Dog—Please!" Lo began the familiar ritual dance, circling the area for a minute as I stood prepared with bag in hand. She made her point and I pick up where she left off, remembering an old rumor about her owner.

Reed, or so it's said, once sent over a surprise package to his friend and colleague, David Bowie. It was the proverbial silver platter, and on it a pile of human excrement, presumably Reed's own. The signature of a fellow artist who disapproved of Bowie's new commercial success? "I *think* he's a friend of mine," Bowie told an audience before singing one of Reed's songs on the final night of the Ziggy Stardust tour.

It had been nearly two weeks of walking little Lolabelle on the wild side of the street, and still I hadn't seen a dime of what was owed me. I hadn't seen Laurie since that first night. She was always at the studio rehearsing when I arrived. I was embarrassed to ask Reed for the money, even though I'd explained up-front that I got paid weekly. After haggling me down on my rate, he seemed to think that since this was a trial period, it was also some kind of free sample. I've had to deal with this sort of wishful thinking many times over the years. Some clients leave you no choice but to ask to get paid, and then to feel you've breached some rule of etiquette by asking. They also insist on wanting nothing but the very best for their dogs—so long as they don't have to pay you for it. Seeing such pettiness, and greed, in my boyhood idol was disappointing, but like I said, you don't really understand New York until you've lived here.

All that time expecting to be paid, I'd jumped through more hoops than Lolabelle would have if she'd run away and joined the circus. The threats about "a single hair on her head" stopped, though, and in some perverse way I was proud to have been on the job longer than any of my predecessors, even if I wasn't being paid. Shouldn't walking the great rock icon's dog be compensation enough? Mr. Reed—I still couldn't bring myself to call him "Lou"—and I seemed headed toward a mutual understanding, and though things were still a bit tense when I arrived promptly at noon each day to find Lo leashed and ready to go, Reed was starting to trust me, as far as a star can ever really trust anyone in this town.

Laurie's tour was fast approaching and I was awaiting final judgment on being worthy to have Lolabelle sleep over. I could safely assume Reed would be making that decision, and today was the big day. If he approved, he'd leave Lo for the night and, "if it works out," I'd be boarding her while they were away.

If only every guy could look down and see his boyhood idol climbing five flights of stairs, sweating profusely, stopping to catch his breath at each landing, and for the pleasure of seeing the humble place I called home. Reed looked up from the third floor—two more to go—Lo's leash in one hand and a big duffle bag in the other. I shouted an apology for living so high. Reed came in and plopped down the bag. As always, my dog Samantha was thrilled to have visitors. Lo seemed to think that Sam was her mother and started licking her mouth.

"So this is where it all happens," I announce jokingly as we sat on my bargain futon that doubled as a bed and a sofa. "My place is what I like to call 'modern on a budget.' It's when you take all your shit and just throw it out." Reed laughed, a little. "I don't even bother with rugs anymore. I've never had fleas or ticks in the apartment, and that's probably why."

Reed looked around, polite enough not to say what a dump my Village artist's pad was. He wore a black leather jacket cut like a biker's, metallic silver lamé gloves he took off as we talked, and aviator shades, mirrored, another trademark. He reached down to unzip the duffle bag and pulled out a sack of puppy kibble, some toys mauled beyond recognition, and a little corduroy dog bed just Lo's size. The trainer had instructed him to include anything that might make the puppy feel at home on her first night away from mom and dad, usually articles of clothing strong with the owners' scents, the stuff of sweet dreams for a homesick pup. Reed pulled out a woman's T-shirt, then a pair of men's briefs, black with "2(x) ist" embroidered on the waistband in white (only the coolest people were wearing these back in 1999).

"These are mine," he said, looking over at the copy of his *Transformer* album—not the CD but the vinyl original I bought back in 1972 with lawn-cutting money—left out as though by accident. "And I want them back."

Why on earth would I want to keep his dirty laundry? Suddenly I remembered something Andy once talked about. Had he lived longer, he might very well have opened a store that sold celebrity underwear. Actually, there were to be two stores, one for undergarments that had been washed, and a second for the dirty, by far the priciest kind. I felt that flash of enlightenment supposed to come when the planets align and you get a glimpse of some eternal truth, when the high and the low are united for the ages and your own little life is imbued with a greater meaning.

Lolabelle stopped licking Sammy's mouth and started to play. For dogs, those two front paws plopped on the floor are an invitation to the dance. My dear, sweet Samantha, the paragon of gentle patience, had helped me bag more than a few clients with her natural charm. She took a full somersault, as she did with me when we were playing, landing on her back, hind legs in front of Lo who was excited beyond belief. Reed and I looked on silently, pleased by the tender scene of two dogs losing themselves in puppy play. The best show in town.

"Dogs are one of the few things that make this city bearable," I said, meaning every word.

"I don't know if I'd say *that*," Reed answered, mesmerized though he was by the two lovely creatures rolling around on the floor, growling and gnawing on each other.

They jumped up and began chasing each other back and forth across the length of my studio apartment.

Reed and I talked for over an hour, intensely as never before, while our two wild-childs ran amuck. We spoke of dog behavior. We spoke of diet and health. We spoke of what gives them diarrhea. We both lit up—though I'd seen somewhere he'd given that up—then we spoke of Tai-Chi, Reed's replacement for partying. We spoke of Japanese brush painting, my own latest pursuit of discipline and concentration that sapped me after a couple hours of turning out the contemplative images of bamboo and mountain streams adorning my cracked-plaster walls. We spoke of my lover who'd died of AIDS, and how I got Samantha soon afterward, then dropped out to become a dog walker. Then we spoke of Lolabelle. Always back to Lolabelle.

I said I understood what it was like to be a nervous parent, that there were only one or two people in all of New York I'd ever trust with my Sammy, and that I was a responsible guy.

"You seem like a responsible guy," he replied, parroting me. The "responsible guy" part seemed utterly out of character and I was flattered.

"Sometimes I just can't bear the look on Lolabelle's face whenever Laurie leaves the apartment," he added on an all-too-human scale, looking like he was about to cry.

Flashback to a Warner Bros. cartoon I'd watched as a kid on Saturday mornings. Bugs and Daffy are going on vacation and burrowing their way underground to get there. They've taken a wrong turn at Perth Amboy and end up, not at Pismo Beach as planned, but in the Himalayan mountains. They run into an enormous "abominable snowman" who wants to crush them both but falls in love with the cute and fluffy little "bunny wabbit." Bugs has no interest in being the monster's pet, and after several attempts to escape finds himself back en route to Pismo Beach where he sits, incognito in dark shades at the poolside, with the abominable snowman, who has followed him and is spilling his guts from a chaise lounge.

Unaware he's talking to the object of his obsession, the monster laments his beloved "bunny wabbit" who got away. All the while, the sun is melting him, until all that's left is a puddle of water, and a pair of sunglasses.

The next morning, Lo and I were in a cab heading across Canal Street where I'd be returning her to Reed's assistant at his sound studio. I'd been told to await further instructions on whether I'd have the honor of caring for her in two weeks when Laurie and Lou left town. On the seat beside me was the big duffle bag packed with all of Lo's things—*all* of them—and on the floor of the cab was Lo, sniffing under the front seat for something.

We pulled up beside the row of cast-iron facades that cut an angle across that strange no man's land where Canal Street tapers off onto West Street, the last creaky old buildings from another era before the river's edge. Outposts built on landfill and overlooking the end of the world, they'd soon to be torn down and replaced with luxury condos.

Lo had picked up the scent of something under that cab seat, and being a digger, was not giving up until she found whatever it was. I reach down and picked her up to find she had something in her mouth. That was all I needed, this dog getting sick on my time, or worse, the poor thing choking on something. I put a finger into her tiny mouth to retrieve the treasure filched from the filthy floor of a New York taxi. Balancing on my index was a fake plastic nail, purple with silver glitter, perhaps left by a prostitute or a guy in drag. Out the window it went.

Inside the office of the sound studio, Reed's assistant handed me a check for forty dollars—the lower rate he'd haggled me down to for boarding—drawn against an account called "Sister Ray Enterprises, Inc." and signed by Reed himself, or maybe not.

I never heard from Laurie or Lou about Lolabelle's next visit. In fact I never heard from them again. I assumed they were shopping around and found someone else. I was also never paid for those dog walks. About a year went by, until one afternoon in the Washington Square dog run a little black, brown and white dog came rushing up to me frantically, jumping on my knees then turning to Samantha and licking her mouth. If this was Lolabelle, then she'd grown, even fattened a bit. Not sure this was the same dog, I reached for her collar and sorted through several tags. There it was, "Lola-belle," engraved on a 3-D candy-red plastic heart.

The guy walking Lo had seven other dogs. He was one of those "multiple walkers," as we call them downtown where they're frowned upon, the ones who only charge five dollars an hour and have phone numbers on their backs.

CHAPTER TWELVE

I was playing fetch with a black Lab named "Tess" at a small private dog run on the Hudson River, and her contracted hour was nearly up. Slobbery tennis balls packed away neatly in a doggy backpack Tess wore with pride, we headed home eastward along quaint brick thoroughfares.

Leaving behind the remodeled riverfront with its scenic bike paths, fake forests, and decorative bouquets of "native" grasses sprouting from breaches in concrete, Tess led me along our established route. Most of the buildings in my neighborhood had been around centuries before I arrived, but now their charming facades were renovated and looking oddly new. The Village was changing so rapidly in recent times of hyper-gentrification that anyone who knew it would scarcely recognize the place after only a short absence. Real estate madness, and an influx of obscenely wealthy colonizers who hadn't a clue about New York, had transformed much of Manhattan into a fortified playground for rich kids—no different from that opulent Upper East Side I'd always loathed, and the slick, up-tight, status-conscious town in Michigan I'd come to escape.

We may have had crime before, but at least we had character. The new New York was a haven for posh suburban-ites who brought their color-coded catalog lifestyles, homo-geneity, squeaky cleanliness, and despite all the "progressive" posturing, their very conservative lives. The far West Village, being verifiably historical and quite beautiful to behold, was among the biggest draws for affluent newcomers seeking se-cure investments and safe spaces to spawn. An old-fashioned setting, it still had the lore of being a milieu where interesting things happened, but to anyone like me with the benefit of hindsight, the Village had been stripped of all the creativity, funkiness and debauchery I knew once thrived behind those flawlessly-restored brownstone surfaces, relacquered front doors, airtight Anderson windows, and historically-accurate railings and lanterns retrieved from warehouses in Brooklyn. Four-figure baby strollers hitched to front stoops like horses, the Times Square light show glaring over the horizon, this family-friendly, corporate version of a village, once you got to know the sort of people actually living there, might as well have been the "Main Street, U.S.A." greeting visitors to Dis-ney World in Florida, or any upscaled old town with a mi-cro-beer brewery and a Polo shop to call its own.

Before anyone now living in Greenwich Village was born, Henry James, a longtime resident but decades-long expatriate, upon a brief return remarked how the New York he'd known was changing, consuming itself, erupting into something new, less for better than for worse. James landed in his former hometown disoriented, a mere tourist, a stranger in a strange land. Rows of buildings had been extracted and supplanted by large, sterile high-rises which, as far as he was concerned, didn't belong. To salvage something of the past, historical commemorative plaques were dutifully affixed at eye level, recording facts like 'So-and-so *used* to reside here between such-and-such dates in a house that *used* to stand here before being demolished.'

That was over a century ago. The hyper-gentrification seen in my lifetime was different. "Preservation," or the illusion of it, was the new style, and to keep the area looking vintage and established, commercial ventures peddling the past went to any length to keep things looking intact, sometimes intimating, ever so slyly, a past that never was.

Like the local outlet of a national chain with windows that advertised, in gold-leaf lettering: "Goorin Bros., Bold Hatmakers Since 1895." That may very well have been true, but not in the Village until just a few years ago when the store opened, not that rich new residents or passing tourists would know the difference. It took some annoying old gadfly like me, a vanishing breed from another era—a *real* anachronism, no fabrication—to remind everyone what was genuine and what was fake.

Or the apparently dyed-in-the-wool Brooks Brothers Black Fleece store, which lasted only long enough to be replaced by another nostalgia trip selling retro-style swim trunks for a mere $128. A bit of true history, off the beaten path of the new luxury outdoor shopping mall that Bleecker Street had become: This same building, prior to 'restoration,' once housed Condomania, the country's first prophylactic store in the early 1990s, an attempt to save lives during the scourge that pretty much wiped out my neighborhood, leaving it prey to developers, and screaming kids in sumptuous strollers.

I used to say, back when so many men were falling, that if I'd been born too late to see my friends come home in body bags from Vietnam, I hadn't been spared the trauma of living with carnage and wondering if I'd be next. How could anything unpleasant have ever happened in such a lovely setting? Residents of these less eventful times, Tess the black Lab and I made our way past precious shop windows warmly aglow with essential oils and olive soaps, shagreen belts and zebra handbags, Paris perfumes, chocolates worth their weight in gold, peasant bread. Vanished were the local grocers, bakers, butchers, shoe repairs, laundries, and diners that had served generations and were now in desperately short supply. If only we'd known, those years we bemoaned the landing legions of Starbucks outlets, how bad the situation would one day become. Starbucks had to share the wealth with several start-up boutique coffee purveyors per block, all vying for tourists who might spread word of their "third wave" beans back home and make them the next international franchise. Each café had its own tight-knit clique of over-caffeinated locals who didn't take kindly to having just *anyone* wander in, proof to out-of-towners of how very special their beans must be. So strong was the competition to impress passersby, that not even the high-end antique shops occupying a stretch of Bleecker for decades could survive the onslaught of Marc Jacobs for men, Marc Jacobs for women, Little Marc (for the invader spawn), handbags by Marc, makeup by Marc, Bookmarc, Marc by Marc—everything, at the time of writing, but Cupcakes by Marc.

Tess and I soldiered past Marc World, Ralph Lauren, a few stray London clothiers, and a string of stores I called "Little France," huddled closely together to distract from rows of grim and vacant storefronts asking astronomical rents but finding no takers. The new Village businesses were the equivalents of flag-ship stores, really, or billboards in Time Square, because there was no way anyone was selling $80,000 worth of Shetland wool sweaters, bench-made shoes, or scented candles per month. Having millions of tourists see their brand names as they passed along old Bleecker, then go online at Christmas time and buy, was worth the investment. Pretensions to local color ended abruptly at Sixth Avenue as Tess and I entered the drab wasteland of palatial bank lobbies, each spanning the length of several local businesses no longer, sometimes two or three banks per block. Interspersed by more vacant spaces that no one else could afford anymore, these temples to money had gleaming glass facades exposing endless expanses of modern leather seating should clients wish to wait—empty day and night without a sign of life, but reminders to passersby of their holdings.

Tess and I passed another row of banks and landed in front of a crooked little shop window, out of place but once used to display old watches or something—I couldn't remember—now covered with a sign for a commercial real estate broker. Above the phone number for anyone interested in renting at the high-profile locale was the company logo. A dog looking very much like Tess, a Labrador retriever, if I knew anything about dogs, was shown in silhouette form pointing stage right, presumably at a bird some hunter hoped to bag. This was an uncharacteristic pose for a type traditionally custom-bred for one purpose: to mechanically retrieve birds *after* they were shot. I phoned the broker's office the next day to learn this was meant to be the owner's own personal pet, the latest hybrid designer breed called a "Pointing Labrador Retriever." Not only would this high-tech hound go after the goods on command, apparently, but would also direct the user toward opportunities. Unlike my poor friend Tess who stood there, still panting after a game of fetch and blissfully ignorant of her obsolescence, this new multitasker was a fitting mascot for the times, a guide dog to passing prospectors with eyes squinting at tiny screens on handheld devices, scavenging the Internet everywhere they walked, perpetually leashed and reachable by text, email, Twitter, Facebook, Instagram—blind to everything I've just described.

There I was, the gadfly ready to sting them into consciousness, the unforeseen Village institution not on their Google Maps, though Google Street View showed my bike parked in various locations at all seasons. Not quite oblivious to all they passed, younger men managed, as a rule, to notice my receding hairline and reached, reflexively, for reassurance that their tufts were still intact. Otherwise, I was off their radar. It had never occurred to me, moving into my fifth-floor walk-up apartment thirty years before, that I might in some distant future become one of those crazy old Village people, the oddballs entrenched in an 1890s building and hard to notice on the street if you weren't looking. Once wild and cocky like me, they migrated here because they didn't fit in back home. Artifacts from other eras, they slowly slid from eccentricity into senility from seeing so much change around them. Most people, who spend their lives in other places that stay more or less the same, aren't forced to witness such cruel and utter decimation of their worlds. New York with its constant stimulation can keep people young, but only up to a point. Then it becomes hard, I myself learned by living here perhaps too long, to keep that original thrill for a fast-paced city that doesn't slow down because you do.

Those cranky, white-haired characters looked lost, though they'd spent their entire adult lives in the Village when I arrived. They wandered the same sidewalks, stopping, starting, staring into the distance. They huffed and puffed in my stairwell, straining with bags from the supermarket down-stairs where they became confused at the cashier and held up the line. They paused to rest on landings as they climbed to collapse in rent-controlled hovels called home since before I was born. Sometimes, when they left their doors cracked for ventilation—only recently has there been enough power in my building to run air conditioners—I dashed nimbly to the top, several steps at once, grabbing glimpses of their ancient nests piled with accumulations of the ages. As they died, their units were gutted and given stark, uniform interiors, clean lines and flush surfaces, uncluttered without a tchotchke or doily in sight, except ironically, all planned for some total visual effect that would be hard to sustain over a lifetime. Before bodies were cold, workers arrived in a black van with sledgehammers and wheelbarrows, an oblong rusting iron dumpster parked on the street below like a sarcophagus receiving intimate remains. Homeless people picked the contents clean, leaving unwant-ed clothing, letters, trophies—family photos, diplomas, cer-tificates of religious rites torn from their frames—all strewn obscenely across the sidewalk for public viewing. This was the fate awaiting many Villagers like me.

If you could pry my fading neighbors from their snail-paced trajectories when they came down to the sidewalk, they were eager, even desperate to share their life stories with any-one who might relay them respectfully. Every morning, Ann, the octogenarian who shared a rusty, wobbly fire escape with me, popped her head out the window and reminisced about the family-owned bakery that used to be across the street, and how much quieter the Village was back then, more like a village. She fed the doves from her window for a half century, chasing away pigeons in those days before they gained public sympathy. Thirty years after Ann passed, I still awoke to the silhouette of a dove through my blinds, or a pigeon still trying to weasel in, as the sunrise came streaming through my window onto West Fourth. No one was feeding them for generations of birds, not since Ann left out bowls of seed for their ancestors, and yet they passed on the word and kept to tradition for no apparent reason.

I wondered if they shared Ann's tales of locals like Anatole Broyard, still writing literary criticism for the *Times* when I arrived, but who, unknown to me, owned a used bookstore on nearby Cornelia Street. Did they carry Ann's messages about obscure Abstract Expressionist painters with whom she'd imbibed, seldom mentioned but considered important in their day? Ann wasn't around to watch the old tavern on the corner become a GapKids, or to see it boarded up briefly, along with blocks of storefronts up Sixth Avenue, on the eve of the Rodney King verdict in case of trouble.

"What the hell do we need so many banks for?" Ann would have asked if told what occupied that corner now.

There I was—I really wasn't supposed to live so long— the last man standing, the oldest tenant in my building. Tourists who wanted to learn about the Village would've been wise to ignore the official tour guides, tourists themselves with their litanies of clichés on Stonewall, Walt Whitman and Thomas Paine. I heard them going on about ancient history, much of it embellished, on Fridays when I asked their audiences to please step aside so I could drag my bag of dirty clothes and wait in line at the only local laundromat left, next door to the house where—yes, I'd heard it a thousand times—John Wilkes Booth tried to recruit a friend to kidnap President Lincoln. Walking west to the next corner, pilgrims landed like homing pigeons, day and night in flocks or solo, to take long-arm selfies with the building used as a front for a popular TV show, actually shot in an L.A. studio, called *Friends*. On the first floor, there used to be a restaurant called The Bistroquet where I treated friends and family for years, since displaced by a very upscale eatery only my new neighbors could afford. Fans of *Friends* stopped me, and my dogs, to ask directions to "Central Perk Café," a fictional hangout they'd seen in many episodes, recreated by Warner Bros. with "working replicas" in cities across North America. No, I assured them with their disbelieving looks, I'd never known such a place. Around the corner, the *New York Post* could've also told them, "Walt Disney did not, in fact, rent at 102 Bedford St. (and neither did Cary Grant). But you could nab this $5750/month one-bedroom."

Painters, poets, novelists, playwrights, conspirators— apart from the architecture, the Village itself had stopped being interesting long before *Friends* ended. Most "creative types," besides the big names already established, had been chased off by real estate or death. About the only "activists" left in the Village, a neighborhood with a history of radicalism, were the radical-chic rich suburban kids who seldom took their signs and slogans far from NYU's manicured front lawn in Washington Square. Visitors didn't believe me when I told them that not even many gay people lived there anymore. The "Big Gay Ice Cream Shop" had until recently been selling cones to the tourists from a truck, and now that they were pegged on a Google map, everyone thought they were a Village institution. They were not. Nobody I knew gay, lesbian or bisexual went to the Pride parade anymore, or the Halloween parade for that matter, both started by locals with vision and talent who fought for causes and made the streets beautiful long before the flat-footed day-trippers overcrowded them with no sense of style. Call us snobs, but survivors stocked up on food and water, locked their doors and windows, or got out of town before the revelers arrived to trash the place and leaned on my bicycle to vomit.

I dropped off Tess the black Lab at her home on West Ninth, picked up dinner at the only decent Chinese restaurant left north of Chinatown, and started the same ascent I'd been making for decades, one step at a time lately. While cameras kept rolling for movies, TV shows, commercials and selfies on the street below, other cameras in my stairwell, in the entryway both coming and going, and wrapping around the front of my building, seven in all, recorded my every move. They'd just been installed by the landlord perhaps to find reasons for evicting old-timers like me who paid lower rents—and sometimes, yes, made money on the side subletting or boarding pets, or had primary residences elsewhere. Constant surveillance from every angle, an intrusion unthinkable until recently, was an effective strategy for turning over populations, not only in my neighborhood, but across the city. This was how they'd ruined New York.

Along with the cameras, my landlord had installed someone downstairs in apartment number thirteen. A bit of research revealed the possible spy worked for a prominent real estate broker and his personal profile said he appreciated "the city's architecture." Was my landlord planning to sell the building? If so, he could ask a better price with fewer "legacies" like me. My new neighbor's specialties were "pre-acquisition" and "development." Did this mean helping to evict me? Perhaps I was being paranoid.

It seemed that after twenty years of boarding dogs in my home and not a word from the landlord, I was suddenly breaking some archaic city heath law against pet sitting no one even knew existed, not until it was mysteriously unearthed and planted in the press. Taking money to care for dogs without a license, or a proper kennel facility, made me a "nuisance," the lawyers could say in court, though none of my neighbors had once complained, in all those twenty years, of days made cheerier by my well-behaved guests who passed, tails wagging and begging for ear scratches, in the stairwell. My clients had never objected, but considered me vital to their dogs' well-being. To them, I was "a lifesaver," "one of the family," "Archie's godfather." Across the city, health inspectors were being sent to search apartments for traces of such abuse—doggy beds, water bowls, chewy toys—to stop this heinous practice of letting beloved dogs, for a modest fee, curl up in kind, familiar homes while the parents traveled, homes away from home that were not, were never meant to be, 'up' to standards for commercial kennels. Slowly but surely, anyone with companion animals in New York could no longer leave their friends with small-time independents like me whom they'd known and trusted for years, sometimes for generations of dogs they'd sent to me for boarding. Instead, they would be forced to pay much higher rates, and to risk their dogs' health, safety, and happiness in small, crowded enclosures notorious for disease, and worse, where days were ended in cages.

The new, law-and-order New York was a place where you could no longer get away with anything unofficial. If you strayed and were charged on a mere technicality, you could be evicted and exiled for good, because real estate prices had barred re-entry to the city for all but the very wealthy. One of my neighbors living across the park, the actor Alec Baldwin, though successful and more accustomed to being on camera than I, had been through similar ordeals with law-and-order, not over dogs but over his bike—though he did have dogs as well. Walking by with his two pups in Washington Square, he always stopped to talk to mine and say how cute "these guys" were. My nice neighbor was nabbed, a couple times, peddling his bike in the wrong direction up Fifth Avenue, an offense traditionally ignored, like jaywalking was in New York, but now suddenly a menace to public safety. He was put in handcuffs, and photographed by the papers, for smarting off. The press had a field day with this arrogant celebrity living in the past and thinking he was above the law. "New York City," he remarked sadly, had become "a managed carnival of stupidity that is desperate for revenue and anxious to criminalize behavior once thought benign." This made the media even madder.

One day I was walking a few dogs past Baldwin's home on East Tenth and ran into something big happening. I knew the apartment building well, having walked many dogs living there, and also having had a torrid months-long *ménage à trois* on a different floor. A mob of media, with mobile units, satellite dishes, harsh lights, and miles of electrical cord, was encamped on the sidewalk out front. This was the second time the bottom-feeders waited at Baldwin's place to harass him, the cops standing by while reporters terrified his daughter trying to leave for school.

One of the "journalists," a young woman, was speaking into a microphone by the entrance and I asked her, matter-of-factly and live on camera: "Why are you doing this to Mr. Baldwin?" She grimaced and tried to keep following the script. Her crew prepared to rush me, but I had some pretty large dogs that day and they stopped to think twice when George the pit bull growled. "You know, he's a real nice guy," I pleaded in my neighbor's defense, despite threatening glares from the crew. "He's a big dog lover, you know." The young woman kept speaking and tried to ignore just another crazy old Village person. "You call this journalism?" I asked, beginning to feel bad because she looked embarrassed and ashamed.

Another "journalist" was stationed on the corner across the street. A balding man caked in makeup, his sport jacket clamped in back and unforgiving light on his wrinkled face, watched nervously as a cameraman counted down the seconds before he went live. They got to "five" and the reporter lost composure when I, the gadfly, stopped to chat as I might with any neighbor on the sidewalk. "Seriously," I asked, "don't you have anything more important to be covering today?" The cameraman, a young, muscular guy, left his post to come at me. "He's doing his job!" he shouted about a second before they went live, bolting back to his camera.

So was I—doing my job.

The reporter explained to viewers of the six o'clock news why he and every other major news outlet were, once again, loitering in front of Alec Baldwin's place. I pretended to walk my dogs away, then circled back a couple times, behind the reporter and into the frame, to taunt the cameraman who watched, teeth clenched, my every move.

ABOUT THE AUTHOR

MICHAEL BRANDOW writes on society, the arts, and canine culture. The author of several books and a sought-after commentator, he has contributed to many publications including the *New York Times*, *Village Voice*, *Town & Country*, *Gizmodo*, *Salon*, *The Bark*, and *Dogs Today*. His works have been listed in *Best American Essays* and he has been profiled in *The New Yorker*'s "Talk of the Town."